Cry for Me, Argentina

Cry for Me, Argentina

The Performance of Trauma in the Short Narratives of Aída Bortnik, Griselda Gambaro, and Tununa Mercado

Annette H. Levine

Madison • Teaneck
Fairleigh Dickinson University Press

Associated University Presses
2010 Eastpark Boulevard
Cranbury, NJ 08512

The paper used in this publication meets the requirements of the American National Standard for Permanence of Paper for Printed Library Materials Z39.48-1984.

Library of Congress Cataloging-in-Publication Data

Levine, Annette H., 1973–
 Cry for me, Argentina : the performance of trauma in the short narratives of Aída Bortnik, Griselda Gambaro, and Tununa Mercado / Annette H. Levine.
  p. cm.
 Includes bibliographical references and index.
 ISBN 978-0-8386-4156-9 (alk. paper)
  1. Argentine literature—20th century—History and criticism. 2. Argentina—History—Dirty War, 1976–1983—Literature and the war. 3. Bortnik, Aída—Criticism and interpretation. 4. Gambaro, Griselda—Criticism and interpretation. 5. Mercado, Tununa, 1939—Criticism and interpretation. I. Title.
 PQ7707.D57L48   2008
 860.9'35882064—dc22

                                                              2007051072

PRINTED IN THE UNITED STATES OF AMERICA

For Robert and Sofía

Contents

Illustrations

All images from the magazine *HUM®* are reprinted with permission from the copyright holder and editor of *HUM®* Andrés Cascioli.

Preface

THE SEEDS FOR THIS BOOK WERE PLANTED IN PAST HISTORICAL traumas, before my time. In a family who barely survived Stalin's and Hitler's grasp, silence often filled the room I shared with my grandmother. I learned to hear the silence and wonder what it was hiding. Though I could not convince my grandmother to narrate her past beyond names of relatives forever lost to her in World War II, I began to understand her history, my history, through literature. In search of an identity in my teens, I clung to Art Spiegelman's *Maus*, Alexander Solzhenitsyn's *A Day in the Life of Ivan Denisovich*, and *The Diary of Anne Frank*.

Writing one's history in the wake of a war-ravaged era rife with trauma is a complex and inevitable process that one must initiate in order to heal and move beyond silence. Inspired by the Madres de la Plaza de Mayo's work for memory and justice, *Cry for Me, Argentina*, is an interdisciplinary study that draws on Latin American, literary, trauma, performance, and cultural studies to analyze the narrative of three Argentine women writers/activists—Aída Bortnik, Griselda Gambaro, and Tununa Mercado—whose work reveals the traumatic repercussions of the Dirty War (1976–83) and cultivates a narrative space for working through the impact of the era: the grave losses of human life (30,000 disappeared individuals), the breakdown of civil liberties, and the ongoing struggles these problems have perpetuated.

The work of these three women emphasizes the imperative to restore the dialogical principle obliterated by repressive authoritarian regimes. Their narrative cultivates a performative space in which they incite the reader to participate in the process of mourning, working toward social justice and healing.

For carefully reading my work and helping me blur disciplinary boundaries in search of literature's function in the aftermath of war, I thank Suzanne Jill Levine, Leo Cabranes-Grant, Ellen McCracken,

11

Patrick O'Connor, and Hiram Aldarondo. The fieldwork I conducted in Buenos Aires has culminated in a project that bridges the fields of literarature, anthropology, and sociology. Research trips to Buenos Aires, funded by generous grants and fellowships from the University of California at Santa Barbara, as well as the Tinker Foundation, allowed me to meet personally with Aída Bortnik, Griselda Gambaro, and Tununa Mercado. I am indebted to these women, who continue to inspire me, for confiding in me during our meaningful encounters. I am grateful as well to Andrés Cascioli for sharing his experiences as editor of *HUM®* and granting me permission to reprint images from the magazine.

Numerous scholars and friends whom I was fortunate to meet in Buenos Aires have had a marked impact on my research. My late friend Mina Fridman-Ruetter was a teacher, translator, and poet, whose Funes-like memory led me to Aída Bortnik's stories in *HUM®*. Betsy Itkin spent tireless hours in the archives with me. Sofía Kaplinsky Guterman's dedication to seeking justice and her personal experience working through trauma have shaped my work. Carlos Feierstein, Fernando Scheitman, Enrique Averbuj, and the Cotton family answered countless questions during many stimulating conversations. I remain inspired by the activism and pledge for justice by *Memoria Activa, las Madres, las Abuelas, HIJOS, Memoria Abierta,* and *Teatro por la Identidad.*

I extend my gratitude to the following mentors and colleagues for their encouragement during various stages of this book: Sara Poot-Herrera, Timothy McGovern, Sandra Lorenzano, Nora Strejilevich, Ryan Alaniz, James McCutcheon, Natasha Zaretsky, Silvia Bermúdez, Susan Derwin, Danielle LaFrance, Jennifer Jolly, Jonathan Ablard, Paul Levine, and David William Foster.

And above all, I wish to acknowledge Robert M. Levine for his many careful readings of my work and for being an unwavering source of inspiration and encouragement during every stage of resesarching, writing, and editing this book.

Cry for Me, Argentina

1. "1976." Photo by author.

1

Boundless Spaces of Grief:
Argentina in the Aftermath of the Dirty War

> The struggle of man against power is the struggle of memory against forgetting.
>
> —Milan Kundera, *The Book of Laughter and Forgetting*

> No thing could ever come to pass that would be so good or pure enough to erase our past. The signs of the offence we suffered would be in us forever and in the memory of those who witnessed, and in the places where the atrocities were enacted, and in our recounting of the events.
>
> —Primo Levi, *The Truce: Survivors Journeying Home from Auschwitz*

APPROXIMATELY 30,000 ARGENTINEANS WERE ABDUCTED, TORTURED, and killed during its last military dictatorship (1976–83), and thousands more fled into exile. As the traumatized country lay in fear, a group of mothers joined together in solidarity and circled the Plaza de Mayo in Buenos Aires—directly in front of the presidential palace—demanding to know the whereabouts of their missing children. The pleas for justice by the Madres de la Plaza de Mayo were initially stifled and many refused to hear them, often calling them crazy—"Las locas de la Plaza de Mayo." Because of their persistence, however, the courage brandished by the Madres echoed internationally and worked to rupture the blanket of silence forced upon Argentina's citizens by the military regime.[1] The oppressive veil, however, was not easily lifted with the onset of democracy in 1983.

Though Raúl Alfonsín, Argentina's first democratically elected president after the Dirty War, pledged to investigate fully and legally address the abuses of the prior regime, his efforts caved in to the pressure to "restructure" the economy and, in turn, the society. One of

15

Alfonsín's first acts as president was to appoint the National Commission on the Disappearance of People, Comisión Nacional Sobre la Desaparición de Personas (CONADEP), to take testimony from victims of abductions and torture, from families and friends of *desaparecidos*, and from other witnesses of Dirty War crimes. Ultimately, Alfonsín only allowed this project one year's time and subsequently, the CONADEP could only document 8,960 *desaparecidos*, not even a third of the missing persons.[2] This collection of testimony was later published in November 1984 as *Never Again, Nunca Más: Informe de la Comisión Nacional sobre la Desaparición de Personas*, and was so widely read that several editions were sold out. In fact, thirteen editions were published between November 1984 and May 1986. The curtailment of the government-sponsored pledge to record testimony, however, put a stop to the "official" process of narrating the historical period and its repercussions.

Alfonsín also called for the investigation and trials of nine ex-commanders of the first three juntas: General Jorge Rafael Videla and Admiral Emilio E. Massera were among the first to be tried. The potential effect of the trials was stunted, however, because Alfonsín feared the destabilizing effects of the prosecutions because of relentless pressure he received from the military. On February 14, 1984, Alfonsín introduced and enforced the controversial Ley de Obediencia Debida, Law of Due Obedience, which pardoned lower-ranking military for their participation in the Dirty War on the grounds that they were merely "following orders." Later, he set February 23, 1987, as the Punto Final, or cut-off date, for all trials related to the Dirty War.[3] Therefore, along with the estimated 400 repressors who benefited from Obediencia Debida, hundreds of torturers and enforcers also had their cases dropped as a result of the deadline set by Alfonsín. Even then, the so-called *carapintadas*, or dissident troops, revolted in 1987 and 1988, taking to the streets in full uniform to protest the cuts in military aid and the trials.[4] On October 13, 1989, President Carlos Menem issued an executive pardon to the convicted ex-commanders of the Dirty War. It is estimated that 280 convicted individuals were set free.[5]

Menem's voice, as it was projected into the public sphere via the media, further denied victims and the nation any space for recognition of their victimization. In June, 1990, he is quoted by Tomás Eloy Martínez in his essay "La Argentina de Borges y Perón," published in the magazine *HUM®:* "The past has already taught us its lessons. . . . We must now look to the future without turning back. If we don't learn to forget, we'll turn into statues of salt" (34).[6] And Diana Taylor quotes

Menem's statement printed in the *Chicago Tribune:* "Argentina lived through a dirty war, but the war is over. The pardons will definitely close a sad and black stage in Argentine history."[7] Whereas studies in post-traumatic healing call for activating memory work and narrative, Menem and his cohorts encouraged forgetting and denied the victims of the Dirty War any sympathy by closing the door on that period of history and granting amnesty to their murderers.

The repression and corruption trickling down from the governing body have compromised the potential healing of the wounded nation. As Fernando Reati suggests in his introduction to *Memoria colectiva y políticas del olvido: Argentina y Uruguay, 1970–1990,* this impunity reactivates the repression of the Dirty War and delegitimizes the identity of the victim: "Today, the presence of the guilty sharing public space with the citizens is sinister. Upon judicially decreeing that there are no perpetrators, impunity reactivates the sinister effect of repression— without perpetrators there are no victims—, and therefore denies once again the reality of the victim" (18). In addition to the menacing presence of Dirty War criminals in the public space of the nation, denial of the genocidal character of the dictatorship by subsequent governing bodies has prevented Argentines from understanding their experience and mourning the losses suffered during the era.

Such political and social pressure—denying discourse and memory with regard to the past in order to focus on rebuilding the national economy—is confirmed by the Brazilian literary critic Idelbar Avelar's view of postdictatorial memory and the imposition of forgetting in *The Untimely Present: Postdictatorial Latin American Fiction and the Task of Mourning:*

> Growing commodification negates memory because new commodities must always replace previous commodities, send them to the dustbin of history. The free market established by the Latin American dictatorships must, therefore, impose forgetting not only because it needs to erase the reminiscence of its barbaric origins but also because it is proper to the market to live in a perpetual present. The erasure of the past as past is the cornerstone of all commodification. . . . The past is to be forgotten because the market demands that the new replace the old without leaving a remainder. (2)

While neoliberal governments working toward competitive market economies believe doing away with the past will pave the road to their economic ventures, the blood spilled in order for these governments to push forward always leaves a remainder in human memory, a traumatic remainder that Carina Perelli calls *memoria de sangre,* blood memory:

"We call *memoria de sangre* the memory that arises from the experience of fear, hardship, pain, and loss so extreme as to turn it into *the* salient fact of the past. *Memoria de sangre* is such a pivotal experience that it becomes the standard of evaluation against which every situation— past, present, and future—will be judged. . . . By its very presence, it determines what is remembered and what must be forgotten" (40). Since it is such a painful past that is being repressed and forced to be forgotten, it inevitably resurfaces powerfully and proves that the past is a reality that will not disappear.

A society of victims, survivors, and witnesses denied bereavement cannot help but act out their relentless traumatic flashbacks of the Dirty War. In "acting out," as the historian and literary critic Dominick LaCapra asserts, "the past is transformatively regenerated or relived as if it were fully present rather than represented in memory and inscription, and it hauntingly returns as the repressed" (2001 70). As this study of Argentine postdictatorship literature will show, Argentina may be read as a nation plagued by the return of the repressed, by unfinished mourning.

The aftermath of the Dirty War's tyranny eludes conventional rituals of mourning and burial. Reati, in *Nombrar lo innombrable*, articulates the violation of the social fabric of the nation that the disappearance of an individual, never to be seen again produces: "The societal impact of the disappearances transcends the acts of death and torture. The collective terror produced by the disappearances, such as the profound psychological wounds caused on the social level, are only understood from the collectively accepted notion of death as 'natural,' related to the meaning of dying, of funeral rites and corporal punishment in our culture" (26). The obliteration of the social understanding of "natural" death eradicates the possibility of conducting culturally accepted and anticipated rituals of burial and mourning. Missing corpses presuppose the inability of cemeteries to serve their "natural" purpose when individuals are abducted and never to be seen again. Jennifer Schirmer astutely posits in "The Claiming of Space and the Body Politic within National Security States: The Plaza de Mayo Madres and the Greenham Common Women": "While cemeteries are bounded, 'timed spaces of grief,' the absence of a body creates painful contradictions: a loss with no end, a bodiless grave, an enclosed space waiting to be filled with a grief that has no closure" (198). The Argentine postdictatorship era abounds with manifestations of what I will call "boundless spaces of grief": an interminable grieving process symbolically practiced by the continued circling of the Plaza de Mayo by *las Madres and las Abuelas;*

the proliferation of groups dedicated to the rescue, collection, and archiving of memory and testimony; the continued search for grandchildren born in captivity and clandestinely given up for adoption; and the production of art that engages the phenomenon of "enclosed space waiting to be filled" in the Dirty War's aftermath.

Such *boundless spaces of grief* manifest themselves in the short narrative of Aída Bortnik, Griselda Gambaro, and Tununa Mercado: Bortnik's short stories are plagued with elliptical textual spaces that draw the reader into a performance of mourning; Gambaro traces the economic and psychological repercussions of the regime while encouraging solidarity and community; and Mercado's writing of her own traumatic entrapment weaves memory and grief into public yet intimate spaces of commemoration, resuscitating the presence of the disappeared. The short narrative by all three women speaks to the imperative of the nation to come to terms with its yet unfinished mourning.

Inspired by the Madres de la Plaza de Mayo's work for memory and justice, *Cry for Me, Argentina,* is an interdisciplinary study that draws on Latin American, literary, trauma, performance, and cultural studies to analyze the narrative of three Argentine women writers/activists whose work reveals the traumatic repercussions of the Dirty War and cultivates a narrative space for working through the traumatic impact of that era: grave losses of human life (30,000 *desaparecidos*), breakdown of civil liberties, and ongoing struggles these problems have perpetuated.

The "otherness" already prescript to trauma, further intensified by pressures to forget the past and focus on the future, leaves the survivors and witnesses of Argentina's Dirty War in a state of "entrapment" that affects not only the individual but also the collective.[8] Because the "hauntingly possessive ghosts of traumatic events," as LaCapra calls them, "are not fully owned by anyone, they affect everyone" (1995 xi). Therefore, trauma should not be treated as solely a possession of the primary victim. For, in so doing, society denies its responsibility of understanding its history and therefore its own identity.[9] It is essential, therefore, to undo this entrapment.

According to the psychoanalyst and child survivor of the Holocaust Dori Laub, "A process of constructing a narrative, of reconstructing a history and essentially, of re-externalizing the event—has to be set in motion. This reexternalization of the event can occur and take effect only when one can articulate and transmit the story, literally transfer it to another outside oneself and then take it back again, inside" (69). This process of reexternalization, however, is a painful one, for the trauma victim must once again face the traumatic event and therefore experience a process of retraumatization. Evidently, many trauma survivors choose silence over narration because of the fear of the potential repercussions tied to articulating the traumatic experience. However, turning a blind eye to past events isolates the primary victim and further perpetuates the repetitive nature of traumatic entrapment, thus leaving the victim with no possibility of engaging with trauma and working through it. In a society where trauma is not openly recognized, a sector is marginalized by and within its own suffering and reduced to silence and endless compulsion to repeat the traumatic event. Moreover, silencing the past does not prevent it from being unconsciously passed on to future generations.

Bortnik's, Gambaro's, and Mercado's narratives speak precisely to the haunting of the past and the need for narration in a society experiencing the crisis of aftermath. I situate their postdictatorship narrative in the "shadow" of the Dirty War because their work is survivor of and witness to this period in Argentine history. As a shadow obscures that which lies beneath it, their stories represent the vast and oblique repercussions—the *boundless spaces of grief*—that the Dirty War has caused: the silencing of the Argentine population, the alienating experience of exile, the haunting of loss, and the scars of deceit and uncertainty. They expose the truths hidden beneath the veil of the immense shadow that is the Dirty War's traumatic legacy, and their work may potentially have a transferential impact on their readers, impelling others to conduct memory work and externalize traumatic experiences.

Rather than dedicate this study to a broad analysis of short narrative in the postdictatorship era and the panorama of authors whose work is representative of the form and themes distinguishing the period, I have chosen to limit my focus to three authors whose work allows me to uncover a particular crossroad in which the literary, the sociohistorical, the cultural, and the performative join. Though their narrative styles are considerably different, Aída Bortnik, Griselda Gambaro, and Tununa Mercado share a relentless dedication to confronting issues of human rights, and their work exhibits a consistent battle to denounce the power relations at work under a fascist regime. Moreover, their writings allow us to understand the ethical imperatives faced by artists in countries ravaged by internal wars. On the basis of the premise that Aída Bortnik began her career as a journalist and has mainly written screenplays, that Griselda Gambaro is renowned as a playwright, and that Tununa Mercado has written primarily as a journalist, I suggest that all three artists are immediately concerned with the reception of their work and its dialogic relation with their audience. Freud's notion of transference, as employed in literary analyses by Peter Brooks, will be helpful in reading these authors' narratives, which, Brooks would argue, "[are concerned with] their transmissibility, of their need to be heard, of their desire to become the story of the listener as much as the teller" (51).

Bortnik, Gambaro, and Mercado are all deeply committed to social responsibility and the desire to raise awareness; it is therefore self-evident that in an era scarred by Argentina's Dirty War, the issues of fascism, trauma, indifference, compassion, and exile reverberate in their narrative. By "deeply committed" I ascribe to the Marxist literary critic Terry Eagleton's definition in his essay "The Author as Producer": "'Commitment' is more than just a matter of presenting correct political opinions in one's art; it reveals itself in how far the artist reconstructs the artistic forms at his disposal, turning authors, readers, and spectators into collaborators" (62).

Furthermore, their "commitment" is one that strives to raise the consciousness of their readers and their audience, fostering my approach to their work as performance. I am interested in their writing not only as published texts and documents that make up a body of literature, but as practices or behaviors that interact with those who read them. Their narrative attends to the crypt that Argentina has become, for many, and opens for the reader a space in which to work through the traumatic history. Considering Mary Louise Pratt's assertion that "literature itself is a speech context," I propose that Bortnik, Gambaro, and Mercado literally initiate the narration of traumatic entrapment and carve a dialogic space. As Pratt asserts in *Toward a Speech Act Theory of Literary Discourse:* "Speaker and Audience are present in the literary speech situation . . . they have commitments to one another as they do everywhere else, and those commitments are presupposed by both the creator and the receiver of the work" (115). As it is acknowledged in the field of performance studies, the circumstances in which the texts were produced and the way in which they are delivered are significant throughout my analysis.[10] Since performances, as defined by Richard Schechner, "exist only as actions, interactions, and relationships" (24), I will consider the performances within the texts, particularly the embodiment and utterance of trauma, in addition to the interactions the texts potentially have with their readers.

The experience of the Dirty War has forever changed the Argentinean landscape. Once-familiar places are now haunted with the terror sowed during the dictatorship. As Tulio Halperín Donghi explains: "Terror has become one of the basic dimensions of collective life, necessarily redefining the horizon in which the experience of each Argentine unfolds: one's relationship with one's country, one's city, and the street where one lives can no longer be the same after years of seeing them marked by death" (71). For this reason, the traumatic repercussions represented in Bortnik's, Gambaro's, and Mercado's work are most effectively reached through the lens of psychoanalysis that works specifically to reach the nature of the crypt and expose its phantoms. Trauma studies, informed primarily by Dori Laub's "Bearing Witness or the Vicissitudes of Listening;" Dominick LaCapra's *Writing History, Writing Trauma;* Nadine Fresco's "Remembering the Unknown;" and Nicolas Abraham and Maria Torok's *The Shell and the Kernel*, will guide my analysis of the use of narrative or "transferential" space in Aída Bortnik's short stories published in the magazine *HUM®* (1981–83); in Griselda Gambaro's volume of short stories *Lo mejor que se tiene* (1998); and in Tununa Mercado's essays, stories, and journal entries: *Canon de alcoba* (1988), *La letra de lo mínimo* (1994), *En estado de memoria* (1998), and *Narrar después* (2003).

Contemporary Argentine literature is largely the product of national trauma and straddles the tense space of memory and forgetting. Representing the traumatic events of the Dirty War is both essential and ineffable. In his introduction to *Memoria colectiva y políticas del olvido: Argentina y Uruguay, 1970–1990*, Fernando Reati writes: "Amnesty, amnesia, anesthesia. These words are particularly important in much of Latin America, but especially in Argentina and Uruguay after the seventies, upon the confirmation of repressive violence, state terror, and reconfigurations of social bodies whose marks are still felt in our imaginaries two decades later. If the seventies were the years of terror, the eighties and nineties are the years of conflict between the will to remember and the attempt to forget" (11). This conflict between memory and forgetting drives Bortnik's, Gambaro's, and Mercado's work. They have all experienced exile during the Dirty War and returned to Argentina with an insatiable need to reconnect with their audiences. While giving testimony to the Argentina they go "home" to, they charge their writing with a plea to acknowledge the importance of memory. They communicate the complex nature of remembering in the aftermath of historical trauma and the haunting presence of the *desaparecidos* in a postdictatorship era that pushes to forget. One could argue that they carry on the legacy of Borges's enigmatic "Funes el memorioso," who, incapable of forgetting after having fallen from his horse, criticizes the first nineteen years of his life:

Me dijo que antes de esa tarde lluviosa en que lo volteó el azulejo, él había sido lo que son todos los cristianos: un ciego, un sordo, un abombado, un desmemoriado. . . . Diez y nueve años había vivido como quien sueña: miraba sin ver, oía sin oír, se olvidaba de todo, de casi todo. . . . Poco después averiguó que estaba tullido. El hecho apenas le interesó. Razonó (sintió) que la inmovilidad era un precio mínimo. Ahora su percepción y su memoria eran infalibles. (170)

He told me that previous to the rainy afternoon when the blue-tinted horse threw him, he had been—like any Christian—blind, deaf-mute, somnambulistic, memoryless. . . . For nineteen years, he said he had lived like a person in a dream: he looked without seeing, heard without hearing, forgot everything—almost everything. . . . A little later he realized that he was crippled. This fact scarcely interested him. He reasoned (or felt) that immobility was a minimum price to pay. And now, his perception and his memory was infallible. (112)[11]

While Borges's irony is more than apparent, there is still in this statement an eloquent assertion of supreme value granted to memory and consciousness. Funes's falling from the horse may be read as allegory for Bortnik's, Gambaro's, and Mercado's relationship with nationhood. The experience of exile and the harsh reality of the Dirty War cause them to reevaluate their past notions of Argentina as home, as national identity. Their works struggle to articulate and maintain memory in an era inundated with postdictatorship policies that strive to put the past aside in order to restructure the economy and society.

Literature produced during and after the Dirty War in Argentina has been an active area of research over the last twenty years. Scholars devoted to examining literature representative of the Dirty War have given particular attention to Ricardo Piglia's *Respiración artificial* (*Artificial Respiration*), Jorge Asís's *Flores robadas en los jardines de Quilmes* (*Flowers Stolen from the Gardens of Quilmes*), Daniel Moyano's *El vuelo del tigre* (*The Flight of the Tiger*), and Osvaldo Soriano's *No habrá más penas ni olvido* (*A Funny Dirty Little War*). In almost all cases, with the exception of Teatro Abierto and Luisa Valenzuela's short stories, research dedicated to this field of study has been largely devoted to novels.

Karl Kohut, in *Literatura Argentina hoy: De la dictadura a la democracia* (*Argentine Literature Today: From Dictatorship to Democracy*), distinguishes three stages in which to situate Argentine dictatorship literature: The first stage precedes the Proceso, and he includes works dating from 1968 to 1976 that reflect the political situation of the Onganía dictatorship. The novels of this first stage, those of Cortázar and Sabato, sympathize with rebellious youth opposed to the brutal repression of the dictatorship and are motivated by a search for a better world. Cortázar's protagonists dream about a socialist revolution while Che, in Sabato's *Abaddón*, embodies a Christ figure. The novels and theater Kohut has chosen as paradigmatic for this grouping reflect a utopic vision.

The second stage collects together the body of what is referred to as dictatorship literature, written during the Proceso. Kohut comments that it is surprising that this period should abound in novels, a genre of "slow gestation," as he calls it. He divides the authors of this stage into three subgroups based upon when they were born and when they began publishing: the first subgroup is made up of works dealing with the Proceso and written by authors born in the 1920s who begin publishing in the 1950s and 1960s.[12] The Sartrian concept of *literatura comprometida*, the political role of literature, predominates among this group of works. The second subgroup consists of those born in the 1930s who begin to publish in the 1960s and 1970s,[13] and the third subgroup consists of those born in the 1940s or 1950s who begin to publish during el Proceso.[14] These last two subgroups are defined by the more autonomous role literature takes with respect to politics. Though politics impacts their work, they tend to coincide with what Mempo Giardinelli says upon defining his own writing: "I don't write literature to be political, nor do I use politics for or in my literature. Nevertheless, I'm a political person. I don't believe in the political role of literature, but rather in political people. . . . And something I find unfortunately inevitable is . . . that politics filter into my writing against my will."[15] Essentially, Giardinelli asserts that what these authors write is representative of who they are, authors personally invested in the political reality of the nation.

For Kohut, Ricardo Piglia's *Respiración artificial* is the most important among this canon of dictatorship literature. The complex construction and sophistication of the novel embody the importance of masking its political intentions. Young Emilio Renzi wants to reconstruct the life of his maternal uncle, Marcelo Maggi, who had written the history of Enrique Ossorio, his wife's great grandfather. In 1850, while living in exile in New York, Enrique Ossorio kept a private diary in which he imagines Argentina 130 years later, therefore situating his futuristic imaginary world within the temporal space of the dictatorship period, 1980. The year 1980 appears as a utopic projection written in the previous century. In one episode, the Polish Tardewski tells

Renzi of his discovery that Hitler, the failed painter, had disappeared in Vienna between October 1909 and August 1910. Tardewski discovered that Hitler had spent those months in Prague, where he had met Franz Kafka. Hitler spoke to Kafka about his political dreams, which Kafka wrote about before Hitler could bring them to fruition. Although it is not said explicitly in the novel, it is implied that Kafka's *Proceso* also prefigures Argentina's *Proceso*.

Kohut's third stage includes literature published after 1985 and is made up of literature not directly dealing with the dictatorship, but in which elements of the Proceso loom: "They generally appear as background or memory" (20).[16] Kohut makes specific mention of the genre of the historic novel, which both breaks with the tendencies of dictatorship literature and fosters continuation of the dialogue about the past. He posits that Tomás Eloy Martínez's *La novela de Perón* (*The Perón Novel*), published in 1985, marks the transition from the dictatorship novel to the historical novel.

Though such a classification system helps scholars establish relationships among various authors of the period, Kohut aptly states that such a system does not satisfy the literary critic, who must "analyze the works in question more closely. These works have in common the resistance that crystalizes in very different ways. The range is very broad and extends from works whose nucleus is the dictatorship to those in which it appears only implicitly or as background" (15). There are indeed many exceptions to Kohut's classification system, and it is difficult to conjecture regarding the direct or indirect literary references to the dictatorship without taking into consideration the overwhelming censorship caused by the fear imposed by the dictatorial regimes. Likewise, the year in which an author could publish was determined by many external factors.

Examining more carefully what Kohut defines as the literature of the Proceso, "stage two" (1976–85), it is evident that the year 1980 marks a significant rupture in the power wielded by the military junta over Argentine authors. There emerges an outcrop of significant literature regarding the Dirty War. Among the works published in 1980 are some of the most recognized for being emblematic of dictatorship literature: Ricardo Piglia's *Respiración artificial* (*Artificial Respiration*); *El libro que no muerde* (The Book That Doesn't Bite), Luisa Valenzuela's first publication since 1977; Ana María Shua's *Soy paciente* (*Patient*); Jorge Asis's *Flores robadas en los jardines de Quilmes* (Flowers Stolen from the Gardens of Quilmes); and Juan José Saer's *Nadie, nada, nunca* (*Nobody, Nothing, Never*). Soon to follow in 1981 are Daniel Moyano's *El vuelo del tigre*

(*The Flight of the Tiger*), the first cycle of Teatro Abierto (Open Theater), and Aída Bortnik's short stories published in *HUM®*.[17]

Though censorship was not officially suspended until November 1983, the military junta began losing its hold in 1980 when the Inter-American Commission on Human Rights circulated a report that was very critical of the Argentine situation.[18] Then began a series of administrative changes among the military generals: in 1980, the junta replaced General Jorge Videla with Roberto Eduardo Viola as president; in 1981, Lieutenant General Viola relinquished his duties to General Horacio T. Liendo, who was then followed by General Galtieri. Though the enforcement of censorship and cultural control by the junta continued, artists began responding to the repression with more vigor and demanding that blacklisting be lifted.

In response to the government's decree that Argentine theater not be studied in universities, playwrights (including Aída Bortnik and Griselda Gambaro) mobilized in creative protest leading to the first cycle of Teatro Abierto. Though the movement was a success, it should be noted that the Picadero Theater, where the first cycle was to be held, fell victim to arson and was destroyed. Violent acts of repression were still a part of the Argentine national fabric. In a desperate attempt to regain public support, the military junta invaded the British-ruled Malvinas (Falkland Islands) in 1982, but in vain. The impossible battle against the British led to further disempowerment and the junta was officially debunked on December 10, 1983, when Raúl Alfonsín was sworn in as constitutional president of Argentina.

The abundance of important critical works published in 1980 has led me to consider this year an appropriate starting point for reading literature in the *aftermath* of the Dirty War. Determining a cut-off date for the *aftermath*, however, is not yet possible. Although a time limit was placed on the collection of testimony gathered for the publication of *Nunca más*, the complex nature of the trauma produced by such a violent era will reach far into generations to come. The works to which I dedicate my research allow us to analyze the representations of trauma from the immediate *aftermath*, the appearance of Bortnik's stories in *HUM®*, 1981, through to *Narrar después*, Tununa Mercado's latest publication in 2003.

I place emphasis on "other" genres in a field where the novel has been a dominant subject of analysis to date by scholars of the literature of the dictatorship era. My study supports the inclusion of short narrative as significant in the body of postdictatorship literature. This genre is significant for its potential to *affect* readers with a sense of urgency, for its having been overlooked in this critical context, and for its great legacy of Argentine storytellers. A scholar of Latin American letters cannot discuss the short story without being drawn to the River Plate region.

Bortnik's, Gambaro's, and Mercado's short narrative does not fall neatly into the predominantly politically charged or revisionist historical accounts that Kohut's stages two and three comprise. Although their work *is* highly political, they convey the emotional pulse of an Argentina in crisis, an Argentina in conflict with its understanding of self and history. At a time when the nation symbolically wrestles with María Elena Walsh's lyrics, "En el país de Nomeacuerdo, doy tres pasitos y me pierdo" [In the land of Idontremember, I take three steps and I am lost], Bornik, Gambaro, and Mercado reiterate the imperative to remember in order to understand Argentine identity in the aftermath and encourage the collective healing of the nation.

2. "Ley de amnistía" ("Law of Amnesty"). *HUM®* 90 (1982): 117.

2

Aída Bortnik's "Tales from the Crypt":
The Disappeared Stories

Mankind has to get out of violence only through non-violence.
Hatred can be overcome only by love. Counter-hatred only increases
the surface as well as the depth of hatred.

—Gandhi

A JOURNALIST, DRAMATURGE, AND SCREENWRITER, AÍDA BORTNIK
(b. 1938), whose accident at the age of twenty echoes Frida Kahlo's
traumatic tramway crash, endured years of physical struggle that
greatly impacted her artistic production. Bortnik's personal history,
which I have learned about firsthand, has not been recorded. Hence, I
will introduce this chapter with this pivotal moment in Bortnik's life
and career, for it drove her to give up her pursuit of an acting career.[1]

At twenty years of age, Bortnik studied law and theater—theater in
order to fulfill her dream of becoming an actress and law in order to
become financially independent. Bortnik's life dramatically changed
when she purchased a bus ticket to visit her parents, who were vaca-
tioning in Mar del Plata. Knowing very well that Condor bus lines was
renowned for accidents, she boarded the bus with the fear that something might go wrong. The highway to Mar del Plata was one lane in
each direction, and it was a night journey. The driver evidently fell
asleep at the wheel and the bus veered into the oncoming traffic, col-
liding head on with a truck. The truck's weight folded into the bus,
killing everyone sitting in front of Bortnik—she sat in the first row of
survivors—and when she was found, she was unconscious and had lost
an immense amount of blood. Bortnik was loaded onto the first vehi-
cle to pass the wreckage, a potato truck. By the time she and the other
injured arrived at the hospital, her wounds were laden with dirt. The
doctor who observed her did not think she would survive. Bortnik

29

recalls that when she overheard the doctor say something to that effect, she opened her eyes and responded: "Te voy a enterrar yo" [I'll be the one to bury you]. The medic apologized and attended to her immediately. She was finally sent to a hospital in Buenos Aires. Her right leg, which was not initially as badly wounded as her left, was infected by gangrene caused by the dirt she was exposed to on the potato truck, and it had to be amputated. Her left leg was so severely ruptured that no one thought she would ever be able to walk again. Bortnik insisted that she would, and her doctor, who attended her night and day, performed a procedure that had been invented during World War I. He managed to salvage her leg after a series of operations. Her left arm had been totally crushed, but she eventually gained enough flexibility so that she could type. She was in bed, totally immobile, for almost four years. Coincidentally, Frida Kahlo was also bedridden for about the same amount of time.

Bortnik did walk again, with the use of a prosthetic limb, but her aspirations of becoming an actress were dampened. She has been confined to a wheelchair since the mid-nineties, when her left leg could no longer support her body. And most recently, in 1999, cancer was detected in her right arm, the one appendage that was relatively unscathed by the accident. During my last visit with her in July 2004, I asked, concerned about her health, how she is doing and she insisted, "Estoy contenta. Sobrevivir no es suficiente. ¡Hay que vivir!" [I am happy. Survival isn't enough. One must live!].

Though this biographical background has not influenced the response to Bortnik's work—in the sense that her personal history is not revealed in her writing—her own struggle for survival and work at post-traumatic self-empowerment have become a textual figure in much of her work. Imagination, creativity, and empowerment (as a nonviolent means to survive oppression and confront violence and hatred) are ever-present tropes in the short stories Bortnik published in *HUM®*.

During the four years Bortnik spent bedridden, she read feverishly. Although she never returned to the university as a student or received any formal degree, she independently studied world literature and theater with the commitment of someone working toward a professional career. Of the many authors she read during those years, Bortnik says that she continually returns to William Shakespeare, Isaac Babel, Luigi Pirandello, and Anton Chekhov. Upon walking again, she soon found herself pursuing a career as a journalist, working for *Primera Plana*, then for *Panorama* while also writing occasionally for *La Opinión*. Finally, she became director of the *Cuestionario* section of *Artes y Medios* until it was confiscated by the military regime and shut down. The knowledge of theater she gained from her years of studying to be an actress persisted, finding its way back into her life as a playwright and screenwriter.

In 1972, Bortnik wrote, directed, and produced the play *Soldados y Soldaditos* (Soldiers and Little Soldiers). That same year, she adapted four chapters of Mario Benedetti's *La Tregua* (Truce) for television, and in 1973 she wrote a film version of the novel. Thus began her professional work in theater, television, and film. Shortly thereafter, she worked on *Una Mujer* (A Woman) and *Crecer de golpe* (Grow Suddenly), directed by Sergio Renán. She also wrote an original screenplay, *La Isla* (The Island), directed by Alejandro Doria, but did not participate in the filming because she was forced into exile in 1976. Bortnik had received threats from the Triple A as early as 1975, by phone and in person. She states in an interview published in *Teatro argentino durante el proceso* (Argentine Theater during the Dictatorship), "They followed me in the street, they flashed weapons at me, they ran me down in cars, not to hit me but to frighten me" (243). Already in 1975 she was prohibited from writing and she appeared to be blacklisted. This type of ban was never made "official" during the Proceso, but it became understood as one's work was continuously rejected and contracts were suspended without explanation.[2] She could no longer work in film, television, or journalism.

Bortnik went into exile and lived in France, and then in Spain for several years. She had written *La Isla* before the military coup, during Peronism. Although the film depicts a love story, the confinement on the island speaks to the restrictions that Argentines were faced with under Perón's government. The director, Alejandro Doria, and his crew began filming *La Isla* while Bortnik was in exile and he requested she return to Argentina briefly to help with the editing process. She returned in 1979 with the intention of spending only a month, but after her first day back in Buenos Aires, Bortnik knew she could not bring herself to leave again. She decided to stay regardless of the danger and remained blacklisted for at least another year.

Bortnik was a key player in the formation of Teatro Abierto, activism by playwrights and actors in resistance to the elimination of the study of Argentine theater in the Conservatorio Nacional de Arte Escénico. Teatro Abierto consisted of twenty-one short works first presented from July to September 1981. Of the twenty-one dramaturges, Bortnik was one of three women involved, alongside Griselda Gambaro and Diana Raznovich. Bortnik wrote *Papá querido* (Dear Father), which was one of four of the short plays selected to continue running for several weeks in the Tabarís theater. Also selected were *El acompañamiento* (The Accompaniment) by Carlos Gorostiza, *Gris de ausencia* (The Grey of Absence) by Roberto Cossa, and *El nuevo mundo* (The New World) by Carlos Somigliana. Bortnik did not participate in the second cycle in 1982 because of differences in opinion with regard to the way it was organized. And in the third cycle of 1983, she presented *De a uno* (One at a Time). Of Bortnik's dramatic work, her participation in Teatro Abierto has been her most notable. Both plays, *Papá querido* and *De a uno*, are strong critiques of authority and speak to the manipulative powers of fascism over an entire population. Bortnik's central message is that everyone is responsible and implicated in the course of history— her work sheds light on society's complicity in the Dirty War, a strong message also portrayed in her screenplay for the film *La historia oficial* (*The Official Story*).

By 1983, Bortnik was well recognized in Argentina. Her screenplay for *Pobre mariposa* (*Poor Butterfly*) won her international acclaim, and she received the Ennio Flaiano award as best international screenwriter. *Pobre mariposa* revealed Bortnik's concern for history in a more direct manner. Whereas her previous work was full of euphemism and allegory, necessary tropes during the era in which she was writing, *Pobre mariposa* does not mask the history of Nazi war criminals arriving in Buenos Aires, the repercussions of such fascist support in Argentina during the years to follow, and the crackdown on the Communist Party and "subversives," evidently foreshadowing the military dictatorships to come.

Today, Bortnik is primarily known for her screenplay of the film *La historia oficial* (1984), an Oscar-winning fictionalized account produced after the dictatorship.[3] The film denounces the compliance with the authoritarian regime on both the individual and collective levels, while also disclosing the important roles the Madres and Abuelas of the Plaza de Mayo played in protesting the Dirty War and demanding that the military regime account for the thousands of disappeared. A central issue in the film, the missing babies born in the clandestine prisons and given up for adoption to families tied to the military regime, was internationally acknowledged as a result of the film's success. Furthermore, *La historia oficial* offers the perspective of a woman coming to terms with the horrific reality of the Dirty War as she moves toward a position of social and moral responsibility, thus situating the film among feminist attempts to recognize the empowerment of women and women's movements.

HUM®

Bortnik's talent and courage in exposing Argentina's "official history" after the dictatorship have been widely heralded. Many, however, do not realize that she also published a series of short stories in the well-known Argentine satirical magazine of the Dirty War era *HUM®*, which David William Foster classifies as the "best forum for sociopolitical commentary" during the Dirty War.[4] In fact, one of the most moving monologues in *La historia oficial* is taken almost directly from Bortnik's short story "Cuatro fotos" (Four Photos), the last of the stories Bortnik published in *HUM®*.

Upon return to Argentina, after having lived in exile during the most dangerous periods of the Dirty War, Bortnik needed work, and more than anything, she longed for a connection with her country. When Andrés Cascioli, founder and editor of *HUM®*, asked her to contribute to the magazine, Bortnik found herself distraught. Although she admired Cascioli's work and had great respect for *HUM®*, she did not feel she could write for a satirical magazine, for the tone of her work would seldom be satirical and would therefore clash with the magazine's objective. Cascioli finally managed to assure her that she could write whatever she wanted, and Bortnik consented. Thus began a publication of thirty short stories that have yet to be reprinted in any other collection.

Since Teatro Abierto first took place from July to September 1981, and Bortnik's first story appeared in *HUM®* in May of the same year, the publication of these stories is relevant to Bortnik's protest of the dictatorship. As Bortnik's participation in Teatro Abierto was a form of activism, her stories in *HUM®* may be read as Bortnik's "coming out" as an activist, for indeed, they are her first attempts at publication in Argentina since she was censored by the military regime. Bortnik has worked to battle the censorship of artists, the repression of creativity and imagination, the fragmentation of society, the negative repercussions of a market-driven economy, and the violent climate of the dictatorship. I read these stories as a means for Bortnik to portray Argentina's sociopolitical climate at a time when the strength of the dictatorship has fallen and the true facts of the *desaparecidos* and Argentina's economic crisis are moving to the forefront.

One must keep in mind that although the dictatorship was in descent, criticizing it in 1981 was still considered dangerous. Though one cannot help but read anything in *HUM®* as harsh criticism of the dictatorship, Bortnik never once uses specific references in her stories; she uses this loaded space of conflict in order to offer "an entrance into a traumatic experience," and to convey a message of compassion, solidarity, and nonviolence to the reader.[5] On the whole, this series of stories works to liberate the reader by opening up a space for reflection, for mourning, encouraging self-awareness and one's potential to effect change by transforming misery into empowerment and therefore working through a traumatic era, working through loss. Although the dictatorship had not yet ended, Bortnik's stories do conjure the losses, as well as look beyond the oppressive era. Therefore, we can consider them as part of a body of postdictatorship literature in accordance with Avelar's definition: "Postdictatorship is taken not only to allude to these texts's posteriority in relation to the military regimes, but also and most importantly in their reflexive incorporation of said defeat into their system of determinators" (15). This definition of postdictatorship, however, does not dismiss the threat of the still ongoing tyranny. How dangerous was it to question and oppose the junta at this time?

Andrés Cascioli and the contributors to *HUM®* were questioning the junta openly and satirically for some years and none of his artists or writers disappeared, although unquestionably, they lived in fear of being kidnapped.[6] Cascioli often had his artists and writers stay in hotels for several days after an edition was distributed, and he went out of his way to defend and protect *HUM®*'s voice.[7] Although the junta confiscated several issues of *HUM®*—those deemed particularly "dangerous" or "subversive"—they did not succeed in shutting down the magazine. One may wonder whether *HUM®* became a means of containment utilized by the junta in order to give oppositional forces a space to vent in a seemingly controlled manner. Therefore, by allowing *HUM®* to exist, the junta prevented a team of artists, writers, and intellectuals from taking other action against the regime.

HUM® was read primarily by Argentines in their teens and twenties, precisely the generation that was being disappeared and targeted by the dictatorship. The magazine began in 1978 and circulated 100,000 copies by 1979; 200,000 by 1980; at its peak, it sold 330,000 copies of issue number 98 in January 1983. Taking into considertation that *Punto de vista* was circulating about 500 copies during the Proceso, and approximately 3,000 afterward, it is evident that topping 300,000 copies in circulation is genuinely extraordinary.[8] As late as 1982–83, the military confiscated issue number 97 of *HUM®*. Even though the dictatorship was soon to end officially and be replaced by presidential elections voting Raúl Alfonsín into office, such control over the press was a means of letting the readers and creators of *HUM®* know that they were still

3. "Prohibido Mirar, Hablar, Escuchar" ("See no evil, speak no evil, hear no evil").
HUM® 98 (1983): cover.

in danger and were being watched. In all likelihood, however, such activity by the regime only sparked more interest in the magazine and led to their most widely distributed issue, number 98, whose cover portrays the military generals who "see no evil, speak no evil, hear no evil": "Prohibido mirar, hablar, escuchar." Clearly, *HUM®* was not afraid to criticize the junta's denial of the Argentine reality.

If Bortnik was not going to write satire or use parody to respond to the dictatorship à la *HUM®*—a seemingly safe and acceptable way to do so since the magazine had already paved the way—how did she recreate the Argentine situation in her stories and manage to criticize the junta without putting herself in imminent danger? David Viñas refers to the Spanish baroque as a means of survival for authors who needed to express their national-historical reality during an era of totalitarianism: "Writing in a baroque style was a way to elude censorship. Language was twisted so the inquisitors wouldn't wring you out on a medieval torture rack." In his opinion, this twisting or linguistic manipulation was the only way to talk about the issues directly connected with the Argentine dictatorship without being killed: "If someone went out on the street on April 3 to denounce the Malvinas/Falkland Islands War operation, he would be lynched. . . . It seems that the cultural production in Argentina during these years could be defined as an elusive, subtle form,of saying things in a way so they wouldn't decapitate you."[9]

Viñas's assessment of the risks posed by writing in Argentina—even toward the end of the dictatorship, when seemingly fewer people were being disappeared and the strength of the dictatorship was flailing—applies to Bortnik's story "Dieciocho años" (Eighteen Years Old), in which she does precisely what he speaks of, not in April but in July. Bortnik denounces the Malvinas/Falkland Islands War in an elusive and subtle manner that detaches it from the subject if read outside the context of the issue of *HUM®* in which it is printed. Only by reading with the objective of linking the short story to Malvinas or by taking into account the paratextual signifiers surrounding the story throughout the issue can one understand its potential.

The physical location—their presence in *HUM®*—of Bortnik's stories is integral to their meaning. Gerard Genette's writing about the paratext, all of the liminal devices or fringes surrounding the principal text at hand, proves valuable in deciphering the messages a text wishes to send its addressee. In his introduction to *Paratexts: Thresholds of Interpretation,* Genette states:

> A literary work consists, entirely or essentially, of a text, defined (very minimally) as a more or less long sequence of verbal statements that are more

or less endowed with significance. But this text is rarely presented in an unadorned state, unreinforced and unaccompanied by a certain number of verbal or other productions, such as an author's name, a title, a preface, illustrations. And although we do not always know whether these productions are to be regarded as belonging to the text, in any case they surround it and extend it, precisely in order to *present* it, in the usual sense of this verb but also in the strongest sense: to *make present*, to ensure the text's presence in the world, its "reception" and consumption. (1)

In many instances, these devices are not produced by the author, but rather by an editor or publisher. Nevertheless, they determine factors affecting the presentation and reception of the author's work. In fact, Bortnik's stories most probably would not have existed if Cascioli had not produced *HUM®* and sought out her participation.

A careful examination of the packaging or "container," as Genette calls the body in which a text resides, of Bortnik's short stories is essential to an understanding of them. *HUM®* offers a platform or a stage for artists and activists to perform their roles of creative protest to oppression. The magazine surrounding Bortnik's stories gives them spatial and temporal location while also situating them in an arena charged with sociopolitical commentary. Thus, the presence of Bortnik's stories plays a role in a theater of criticism directed at the Dirty War. The audience, the readers of *HUM®*, are aware of the functional role of this publication and therefore read with the sociopolitical circumstances in mind. I argue that the reader, as well, is an accomplice and yearns to participate in this charged arena by purchasing and reading a publication considered subversive and constantly called into question by the regime. Satire, by its very definition, demands an active reader who understands the nuances of the various registers of criticism and parody. The informed reader shares a body of knowledge and critical perspective with the satirist. The reader's demand for such a publication further encourages the performance of satire and protest directed at the authoritarian structure of power.

"Dieciocho años"

The publication of "Dieciocho años" in issue number 86 of *HUM®*, which can be considered the "stage" or "theater" in which this story performs a key role, unquestionably situates "Dieciocho años" in a relationship with the subject of the Malvinas. Issue number 86 conjures the tangled military offensive on its very cover, where the illustration features three generals with their hands restrained, unable to move, and

4. "¡Unidos es más difícil!" ("Together it's more difficult!"). *HUM®* 86 (1982): cover.

the headline "!Unidos es más difícil!" [United is more difficult!] evidently mocking the disorganization and clashing ideals among the three branches of the military. The statement also carries a double meaning and implies that it is also more difficult for the military to rule when civilians are united in protest against them.

The illustration on the back cover conveys the impending doom of the situation at hand, one that affects all sectors of society: daggers hang suspended from a gloomy purple sky and the caption reads "¿Qué opina de la situación actual?" [What do you think of the current situation?]. The Dirty War targeted artists and intellectuals, left children orphaned, dragged young men into a battle they were not prepared to fight, planted fear of a large-scale war, and further drained the economy.

The inside cover also calls the war into question. The two-page illustration mocks the discord among the military forces and portrays the absence of the people, whose support the regime hoped to gain by defeat-

5. "La situación actual" ("The current situation") *HUM®86* (1982): back cover.

6. "La junta y el pueblo" ("The junta and the people") *HUM®* (1982): inside cover.

ing the British and reclaiming the Falkland Islands. When one of the three generals, seated at a table reserved for *la junta*, tells a fairylike woman, dressed in colors of the Argentine flag, blue and white, that he is concerned about the absence of his colleagues, she retorts that what worries her more is the absence of the people, *el pueblo*, who should occupy a much larger chair and deserve his attention. The significance of "el pueblo" collapses the definition of both the nation and the people who populate it, further emphasizing the absence of unified support to back up the military offensive.

Criticism of the military junta's decision to reclaim the Malvinas from the British, in a desperate attempt to regain strength and support from the Argentine masses, continues to be fodder for commentary through-out this issue of *HUM®*. An article entitled "La mano negra en las Malv-inas" (The Black Hand in Malvinas), by Enrique Vázquez, is accompa-nied by a survey in the lower-right corner of page eight poking fun at Argentina's repetitive history of dictatorship and military coups. Ques-tion three asks, "Who do you think has more right to govern? A) A mil-itary soldier; B) A farmer; C) A military farmer; D) You?" Question four: "What is the Constitution? A) Something written by ancient Argentines; B) A collection of Creole poetry; C) A science-fiction novel ; D) A train station?" Question six: "How long do you think the Constitutional government will last? A) Six years; B) One year; C) Six months; D) Half an hour?" Undoubtedly, *HUM®* deserves significant attention for its uncanny "humor" during such a violent era and rightly won an interna-tional award for best satirical magazine in Forte de Marmi, Italy, in 1983.

Turning the page, we find Bortnik's "Dieciocho años" and adjacent to it, a caricature of a soldier: he is holding a rifle, toes sticking out of a torn boot, a slingshot hanging from his belt, and a flower sprouting from his helmet. The caption mocks the headstrong unilateral decision by the military to proceed with a battle they could not possibly win: "We lost, but it doesn't matter . . . competing is what counts." With such preamble and pretext surrounding Bortnik's story, her elusive style and metaphors have nowhere to hide. The wide hole the protagonist of "Dieciocho años" digs and then jumps into is easily recognized as a trench, and the heavy object held in his frozen hands must be under-stood as a rifle. Should one read or skim the magazine from cover to cover, "Dieciocho años" continues to pick up signifiers that call atten-tion to the Malvinas War, fill the elliptical space of Bortnik's story, and give shape to its metaphors.

A full-page comic by Marta Vicente entitled "Cuántos" (How Many?) and an article about Malvinas by Luís A. Frontera entitled "La

7. "¿Está Ud. capacitado para votar?" ("Are you ready to vote?") *HUM*® 86 (1982): 8.

8. "Perdimos" ("We lost") *HUM*® 86 (1982): 10.

9. "Dieciocho años" ("Eighteen years old"). *HUM*® 86 (1982): 10.

10. "Cuántos" ("How many") *HUM*® 86 (1982): 36.

11. "Equipamiento obsoleto" ("Obsolete equipment") *HUM*® 86 (1982): 37.

más terrible historia jamás contada" (The Worst Story Ever Told) are accompanied by a caricature in the lower-right corner.[10] In Vicenta's comic, a young boy wearing a helmet, with a gun propped on his shoulder, asks his grandmother, who is knitting, "How many generals are there?" She is uncertain but suggests "Two-hundred." The boy subtracts the seven generals who have already been military presidents and says, "193 more military presidents until the civilians can take over!"

The illustration accompanying Frontera's article features a soldier in knight's armor saying, "What bothers me most, Edelmiro, is that they go around saying we went off to fight in the Malvinas with obsolete equipment!" And indeed, the ten thousand soldiers who were basically rounded up overnight and sent to Malvinas were ill equipped with outdated weaponry and insufficient supplies, training, and clothing to survive, let alone fight during a frigid Patagonian winter.

The failure of the military, due to its decision to wage an impossible war without proper training or equipment, is a consequence of a tyrannical vision portrayed on page fifty of this same issue. A general speaks into the microphones, insisting with fists clenched: "Some people, who remain anonymous, accuse me of torturing my enemies, of violating human rights. . . . That's false! They don't have any evidence. And furthermore, none of my enemies are human." Though ridiculing the mindset of the military, this drawing exposes the fascist extremism that perpetuates the violence of such regimes, not unlike national socialism. Such ideology is constructed on the concept of the irreversibility of evil, thus promoting a complete extermination of whatever forces or characteristics are deemed to be so.

Significantly, this caricature appears within a nine-page interview of the winner of the Nobel Prize in peace, Adolfo Pérez Esquivel. Known for his work and life among indigenous populations in Central America and his dedication to helping poverty-stricken communities, Esquivel was imprisoned for two years during the Dirty War. He founded the Service for Peace and Justice, Servicio de Paz y Justicia (SERPAJ), and supported nonviolent responses to tyrannical forces. His prescription for an Argentina plagued by continuous military occupation is one that empowers individuals to retain their freedom despite the oppressive nature of the governing body they must endure. Esquivel is particularly concerned with the future of education and the media. He states: "Institutions should return to their roots. Education, the media—that no longer accomplish their fundamental objectives—should not only be informative, they should be formative: forming free men and women so they can exercise the right to liberty, to life, to their own essence as

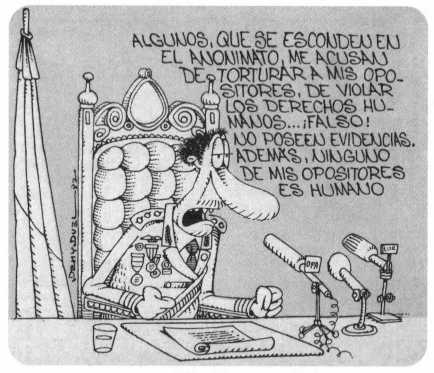

12. "¡Falso!" ("False!"). *HUM®* 86 (1982): 50.

human beings and to their own essence as communities" (45). This idea is particularly significant when reading Bortnik's stories as she repeatedly sends this message to her readers, especially in "Un cuentito" (A Little Short Story), "Tomás el ortodoxo" (Tomás the Orthodox), "El corazón de Celeste" (Celeste's Heart), "Diferencia" (Difference), "Hagamos una lista" (Let's Make a List), and "Oferta" (Sale). Thus, Esquivel and Bortnik are contemporaries working to a similar end and Bortnik's work may be read as a bridge between art and activism.

The visual landscape of issue number 86 of *HUM®* surrounds "Dieciocho años" with antiwar performances directed primarily at the military leaders who have dragged a nation into demise with them. Bortnik's story, however, situates the reader alongside a young soldier and recreates the vast and cold terrain of the Patagonia. The story begins:

Primero cavó ese pozo ancho y después saltó adentro. Y desde adentro levantó la vista y casi hizo una sonrisa mientras asentía para demostrar que había comprendido y repitió sí señor. Apuntó hacia lo oscuro y trató de mantenerse alerta y de no pensar en el frío (11).[11]

First he dug that wide hole and then jumped inside. And then he looked up and almost smiled while nodding to show that he understood. And he repeated: "yes sir." He aimed into the darkness and tried to stay alert and not think about the cold.

Though the protagonist's "yes sir" and the action of pointing into the darkness while trying to stay alert despite the frigid weather provide a military-oriented context to the story, the ambiguity of the wide hole that the protagonist digs and jumps into is dispelled by the sociohistorical context provided by the paratextual elements surrounding the story, signifying the trenches of the Malvinas War.

Using a repetitive device, Bortnik draws the reader into the trench from which the soldier never ascends:

Solamente tenía algo pesado en las manos heladas. Quiso despertarse y salir de allí, pero no podía. Pensó que era otra vez un sueño de miedo. Pero no era un sueño. Nunca más salió de ese pozo que él mismo había cavado. Nunca más volvió a hacer una sonrisa, ni a asentir, para demostrar que había comprendido, ni a decir "si señor". Nunca más le contó sueños a su hermana, ni ayudó a su padre con la cosecha. Nunca más volvió a besarlo una mariposa.

All he had was something heavy in his frozen hands. And he wanted to wake up and leave that place and he couldn't. And he thought it was another scary dream. But it wasn't a dream. Never again did he leave the hole that he himself had dug. Never again did he crack a smile or nod to show that he had understood, nor did he ever say yes sir again. Never again did he hear talk of dreams to his sister or help his father with the harvest. Never again did he kiss a butterfly.

By descending into the trenches where innocence, youth, and dreams are forever buried, Bortnik offers the reader an entrance in which to engage with loss and the catastrophes of war, an opportunity to mourn. The repetition of *Nunca más*, "Never again," the phrase uttered by world leaders after the genocide of the Holocaust, asserts the failure to prevent such massacres. The humanization of the soldier, who is also a son and a brother, works to draw sympathy and invite the reader into the transferential space of the crypt, to mourn for the young soldiers killed as a result of the military intervention, to mourn for the thousands of *desaparecidos* and the consequences of war.

After affecting the reader with the tragic reality, the story moves on to the reader's responsibility to remember in order to keep this history alive and not relegate it to the forgotten archives. "Dieciocho años" ends with an illocutionary statement by Bortnik, a technique she uses in several stories, insisting that the reader not forget the young soldiers whose lives have been sacrificed. The final sentence is "Y si alguna vez llagamos a olvidarlo, que todos aquellos que cumplan dieciocho años, nos lo demanden para siempre" [And should we ever forget him, may we be forever reminded of him by all those who turn eighteen years old]. Thus, "Dieciocho años" confronts the violence and losses suffered during the Dirty War—of which the Malvinas War formed part—with an appeal to memory as a means of nonviolent response.

Effect is precisely what Bortnik sought in the urgency to raise the awareness of her readers, to promote change and resistance within the public domain. As we can see by the brevity of her story—all but one of the thirty are restricted to a page of narrative space—she works to disseminate her message with a sense of immediacy. The stories are also somewhat rhetorical, and her use of illocutionary statements makes it evident that Bortnik was trying to effect change among her readers, among people in general. While *HUM®*'s satire ensures the perform-ance of politics within the public domain, Bortnik's stories work to engender the performance of mourning denied by the political agenda of the dictatorship and commodification encouraged by transnational agendas.

LOS CUENTITOS

Bortnik has not wanted to reprint the *cuentitos*, short little stories, pub-lished in *HUM®* because she believes they should not be read outside the context in which they were written. She does not want them to be judged soley as literary works, that is, outside their political context. However, should they remain hidden in the archives and not discussed, they will suffer an archaeological death and become another contesta-torial body that has been disappeared and silenced. Just as Bortnik emphatically calls for the memory of all young soldiers killed in the Malvinas War, my goal is to resuscitate this collection of short stories, which has remained in the literary trenches of the Dirty War, and reveal its value as a site of activism within postdictatorship literature. Since the stories have been out of circulation since they were published, and no known published criticism of them exists, I provide plot summaries as I explicate them throughout this chapter.

For Bortnik, who had been blacklisted in 1975 and living in exile in Europe, the short stories she wrote for *HUM®* were her first contact with the Argentine readership for several years. When Cascioli asked her to submit a short story every fifteen days, Bortnik once again had a lifeline, a means of communication with her country and her audience. Written in "journalistic time," quickly, and with the objective of a journalistic piece, to draw in the reader and inform, these stories also go beyond the informative function of journalism in that they induce a performative function of empowerment, linking literature and activism. While the Madres de la Plaza de Mayo circulate, promote nonviolence, and demand their children be accounted for, Bortnik's stories encourage people to look within their cores and liberate themselves from their oppressive surroundings. The transferential effect of these stories, as seen in "Dieciocho años," impels the readers to activate memory.

Upon reading them, one must understand both the great risk Bortnik felt she was taking by publishing them and her strong desire to communicate with her readers. The *cuentitos* carry a sense of urgency and are very brief. Her use of language and literary techniques to synthesize each story creates a compact yet resounding presence within *HUM®*. According to Bortnik, these stories were direct products of what she was experiencing in Argentina at the time. She wrote about personal experiences, things she read, heard, discovered, and she immediately worked to disseminate that experience/message to a larger audience. The *cuentitos* are also somewhat rhetorical and her use of illocutionary statements, such as the one at the end of "Dieciocho años," makes it evident that Bortnik was trying to effect change among her readers, among people in general. They belong to a body of what Idelbar Avelar calls postcatastrophe literature, which: "reactivates the hope of providing an entrance into a traumatic experience that has seemingly been condemned to silence and oblivion" (10). They do not leave the reader in an introspective state, but they impel the reader to work through the traumatic hardships of the era and to gain a critical distance in order to work toward social justice. The stories urge the reader to restore the qualities that fear and silence imposed by the regime nearly abolished: solidarity, intellectual and artistic freedom, compassion, empathy, and memory.

Bortnik's stories were circulating toward the end of the dictatorship. Although the fall of the military regime was imminent, censorship and blacklisting were still in effect, and therefore, her stories were shaped by the era. In fact, once the dictatorship had officially collapsed, Bortnik no longer felt the need to write them. *HUM®* also lost many of its readers and with the onset of democracy and the Alfonsín presidency had difficulty finding an audience, or even at times a muse, for its striking satirical tone. Though Bortnik's stories are seemingly lacking in spatial and temporal specificity, as shown in my paratextual analysis of "Dieciocho años," their insertion in *HUM®* surrounds them with the harsh sociopolitical context of Argentina during those years. Even though Bortnik makes no direct reference to the Dirty War in the stories, the dictatorship era is evident in their context and content. She conveys a message against the dictatorship and all forms of power and ignorance that feed it.

Of the thirty short stories Bortnik published in *HUM®*, I will discuss twenty, those that are the most performative in the way they straddle art and activism—activism in that they carve a space for mourning and work to infect readers with awareness and motivation to effect change within themselves and their surrounding environment. Bortnik's evaluation of human nature and encouragement of solidarity in her stories are a result of a reality fragmented by the fear and violence of the era, which has isolated members of a community and led to profound disillusionment. The *cuentitos*, as Bortnik calls them, are her attempt to heighten awareness about the violence, poverty, insidious nationalism, isolation, and censorship caused by the dictatorial regime. The stories work to remind the reader of humans' penchant for power, greed, and violence while they emphatically assign ownership to the reader, via illocutionary statements, to take responsibility for one's actions, to question, to remember those who have been killed, and to respond to hatred with nonviolence so as not to repeat the same crimes of tyranny wielded by the oppressors.

The brevity of each story is ironic because each touches on universal existential issues and principles. In this sense, their value far exceeds their physical length. Calling them "cuentitos" (short little stories) is deceptive—the reader is prone to approach them lightly. The distinction between author and narrator is blurred by narrative devices and paratextual elements. Each story is accompanied by a picture or caricature of Aída Bortnik and her full name is printed beneath each one.[12] This authorial function directly places responsibility for the text on Botnik herself. The author does not vanish from Bortnik's stories. Further, she often writes herself and the reader into the text by using the first-person singular and plural, *I* and *We*, and the second-person singular and plural *you* addresses. The difference between fiction and reality is also blurred by her introduction to readers as a journalist. Above the appearance of Bortnik's very first story published in *HUM®*, in May 1981, appropriately titled "Un cuentito," the editor has added a paratextual note: "Aída Bortnik is an excellent journalist, as she proved years ago in *Primera Plana*. Busy later with other tasks, equally successful, we pestered her to come back into the fold. Our insistence lasted for months. We finally tired her out and won her over, and she has come to tell us (31)." By identifying the author as journalist and noting her work in *Primera Plana*, the editor influences the readers' expectations and Bortnik's *cuentitos* become immediately linked to the social reality in which they are written. Were she introduced as an author of fiction, the readers' expectations would be different. In Brechtian fashion, the deliberate construction of the stories is not concealed from the reader; therefore, the reader's critical judgment remains alert. Moreover, situating Bortnik's texts in a social reality that the reader also inhabits, implicates the reader in or connects him or her to the text more intimately. The reader, encouraged by narrative devices such as ellipses and illocutionary statements, also ascribes meaning to Bortnik's stories, therefore becoming an authorial collaborator.

"Un cuentito" is an appropriate point of departure in order to set the tone for her subsequent stories published over the period of the next two years. The body of the text consists of six main paragraphs, each one beginning with "Cuando éramos chicos" [When we were kids]. This first-person plural address speaks to Bortnik's desire to communicate with her readers and insert herself within a community that she works to impact. Each paragraph of "Un cuentito" enumerates and questions the restrictive societal norms imposed by the government, the media, and the educational institutions. The story touches specifically on the following topics: history and the understanding of war, excessive devotion to and respect for elders, patriotism, strict gender roles, sexuality and marriage, loyalty and friendship. The story questions each of these themes while also leaving an elliptical space of reflection for the reader.

Each paragraph then closes with "Pero esto es otro cuento" [But that's another story]. These narrative strategies release the confining borders of the text and multiply the breadth of this "cuentito," which is much more than one brief short story. The final paragraph reminds the reader of the naiveté of the belief that following these norms would eventually lead to a fulfilling life. Bortnik retorts: "Y la madurez es ahora, y yo no sé a ustedes, pero a mí, a este banquete nadie me ha invitado" [And these are the golden years, and I don't know about all of you, but no one invited me to *this* banquet], thus clearly situating the story, the reader, and the narrator in the social reality of 1981 and expressing disillusionment while criticizing the Peronist era. Bortnik places blame on strict social norms dealing with definitions of gender, sexuality, nationhood, religion, and etiquette, as precursors to the military dictatorship and the violence, fear, and censorship that now abound. Evidently, Bortnik is concerned with the way power is internalized through discursive practices that subtly integrate ideology into the collective social fabric. She connects directly with the reader and impels the reader to question the seemingly innocent precursors to the dictatorial oppression. Then, playfully, she ends the story with " yo no sé a ustedes, pero a mí me parece que este cuento no se ha terminado" [I don't know about all of you, but I don't think this story has ended], asserting the need to grapple with all of the issues introduced in the story and suggesting that these problems are ongoing.

The criticism Bortnik lays out in "Un cuentito" finds its way into all of her stories published in *HUM®*. Many of them follow similar narrative strategies of repetition and ellipses that both increase the momentum of each story and give the reader space for introspection. I have thematically grouped these stories under the following subheadings: (1) Identity and Disenchantment, (2) Violence and Memory, (3) Empowerment and Nonviolence. I address these themes with respect to the sequence in which they were published, with the exception of the final story Bortnik published, "Cuatro fotos," which I have decided to leave for last but would most appropriately be considered under the subheading "Violence and Memory." I have chosen to take the story out of its thematic grouping in order to respect Bortnik's choice to make this the final story she submitted to *HUM®*. Moreover, her decision to adapt this story in an important dialogue of the film *La historia oficial*, produced several years later, further qualifies "Cuatro fotos" as a short story that continued to resound for Bortnik in the postdictatorship period.

IDENTITY AND DISENCHANTMENT

Bortnik's preoccupation with the perception of women, and women's perception of themselves, is evident in the first two stories that follow

"Un cuentito": "Ella y los hombres" (She and Men) and "Ani-Nú y la belleza diferente" (Ani-Nú and the Different Beauty). She takes a stance described by Jean Franco in *The Decline and Fall of the Lettered City*: "Like many French feminists, many Latin American women writers understand their position to not be so much one of confronting a dominant patriarchy with a new feminine position but rather one of unsettling the stance that shows gender power/knowledge as masculine" (57). Bortnik discloses the masculine-centered genealogy of power and knowledge only to debunk it by exposing its negative impact on women's understanding of their own identity in "Ella y los hombres," the inherent marginalization brought on by authoritative structures of power in "Ani-Nú y la belleza diferente," and the subsequent loss of individuality, creativity, and capacity for critical thinking in "Tomás el ortodoxo."

"Ella y los hombres" is written in ten paragraphs, each beginning with the age of the protagonist/subject: when she was five, then fifteen, twenty-five, and increasing successively by increments of ten years until reaching ninety-five. At each stage of her life—as a child, a girl, a woman—she contemplates the men she loves and upon whom her gaze is fixed as they form the center of her universe. As she gets older, the men she falls in love with every ten years have different approaches to life and take on different physical forms; their outlooks on life vary from one another, and she uses similes to describe each man's character: like a mountain, a sword, an ocean, a wind, a rock, a book, a melody, a pathway, and a god. Her position remains on the periphery, as one of outsider and observer—the men are always the objects of her attention.

Only later in her life, upon meeting a ninety-five-year-old man, the only one she does not fall in love with, the one who "era nada más que un hombre" (42) [was nothing but a man], does she take a moment to analyze herself. He is a weak, practically blind man who almost never speaks but is the only man to ask her who she is. He makes her think about her own identity and she realizes that she has never given it any thought. She had been a spectator in a world where the performance of male gender was supreme and she never centered her attention on herself. Bortnik's statement works to unsettle this male-centered tradition and give women a space to discover their own potential. By attending to the absent female subject, the woman who is invisible to her own self (only seen by the blind man), and by conjuring the importance of her presence, Bortnik fulfills an objective suggested by Amy Kaminsky in *Reading the Body Politic: Feminist Criticism and Latin American Women Writers*, that feminist critics attend to "making visible the invisible, the continued life of those who have been murdered, the appearance of the disappeared, the testimony that makes the whole the body of the tortured . . . presence in the face of erasure and silencing" (25). Bortnik's subsequent stories continue this rite of unveiling that which has been made invisible by societal pressures and political agendas.

Bortnik's story shows that women's true identity is not understood because, in most instances, their gaze has been directed at male models. And, in a social hierarchy where men are the authority, women and those who do not perform certain imposed definitions of class, race, and sexuality are often relegated to the margins. Such is the theme also in the third story, "Ani-Nú la belleza diferente." Ani-Nú is an animal of enigmatic nature and is repeatedly told who she is by her family or by the guards who control the grounds and the animals that live on them. Her inability to perform the identities prescribed to her—elephant and donkey (symbolic of the United States' bipartisan government—elephant = Republican, donkey = Democrat—and perhaps a critique of U.S. intervention in favor of military intervention in Latin America) becomes problematic and she is pursued by the guard who "didn't tolerate misdemeanors" (37). Her identity becomes a "fault-line" eluding prescribed definitions and inspires fear and intolerance in a society of rigid norms. In this sense, Bortnik accentuates the "in-between" spaces defined by Homi Bhabha as "the terrain for elaborating strategies of selfhood—singular or communal—that initiate new signs of identity" (1).

She flees the guard's "terrible persecution." Suddenly, this animal world is dictated by intolerance and violence, serving as allegory for the dictatorial regime. Ani-Nú is a subversive element until she escapes to the "Land of Strange Animals" and she longs to be allowed into the group of "Creatures Too Strange to Belong in the World." Though crossing the barrier will separate her from her family, it is only among other marginalized animals, perhaps in exile or among a guerrilla group such as the *montoneros*, who were brutally hunted by right-wing Peronism, that Ani-Nú can find happiness. Though she is isolated from the repressive society she was born into, it is suggested that among the other "strange creatures" she will find solidarity and tolerance as the story ends: "Entonces, por primera vez en su vida, Ani-Nú se permitió el goce del viento en la piel demasiado sensible mientras corría como si volara, hacia su felicidad" [Then, for the first time in her life, Ani-Nú allowed herself to savor the pleasure of the breeze upon her ever sensitive skin while she ran as if she were flying, toward her happiness].

Had Ani-Nú been able physically to conform to being an elephant, donkey, or whatever she was told she was, she would have been an accomplice in the shaping of a controlled or imposed identity, similar to Tomás in "Tomás el ortodoxo." In this story, which appears in the issue of *HUM®* that follows "Ani-Nú y la belleza diferente," Bortnik makes a strong statement against complicity with society and with imposed norms. She traces the progression of a man's life, from his early childhood to his death, and his compliance with rules and what is expected of him. Again, Bortnik uses a progressive repetitive device as in the previous stories. Here, she uses a series of adjectives to describe Tomás's character as she marks the stages of his life. The five paragraphs that trace Tomás's life begin with "Tomas was a very neat young boy; a very disciplined young man; a very organized man; a very methodical husband; a very rigorous father" (32). Each paragraph then speaks of how diligent Tomás was at fulfilling his duties, so much so that he never developed his own personality or knew exactly what it was he was doing and to what end. He never does anything "out of line": "Nunca preguntaba demasiado, nunca pedía demasiado, nunca curioseaba demasiado" (32). [He never asked too many questions, never requested too much, never wondered too much.] Tomás was so worried about doing everything just the right way that he never concerned himself with the meaning of his actions or their consequences. Tomás "estaba tan preocupado por ejecutar todas las obligaciones de la paternidad que nunca pudo conocer a sus hijos. Tomás era un padre al que no inquietaban la frustración de sus sueños ni la posibilidad de una guerra." [Tomás was so worried about fulfilling all of his paternal obligations that he never got to know his children. Tomás was a father who was never bothered by the frustration of his dreams or the possibility of war.] He is the quintessential regimented and obedient citizen who follows orders and would make the perfect soldier. The story ends with the judgment of the Lord after Tomás's death. The Lord recounts Tomás's life and tells him that all he has contributed is empty devotion and says that he is the only unforgivable failure of Creation: "un hombre que no cuestiona" [a man who does not question].

The Lord's judgment is particularly striking as it positions the reader in Tomás's place by using the second-person informal *you* address, thereby forming a dialogic relationship that implicates the reader. Likewise, it is an insertion of Bortnik's own voice and her disappointment with humans' tendency to serve obediently or fulfill certain roles without questioning them. Hence, Bortnik is criticizing the compliance of

Argentines who have not questioned fascist ideologies and the role of the dictatorship. She later counters this negative criticism of human nature with stories such as "El corazón de Celeste" and "Buscando," which I will address in terms of the theme of empowerment.

DISENCHANTMENT

It follows that Bortnik should criticize the growing commodification, fomented by the large corporations, that has been largely backed by the Argentine military.[13] When then-Colonel Perón became head of the national labor department in 1943, he began enforcing his earlier ideals of a military led program of industrialization.[14] Thus, it is no surprise that commodification in Argentina carries fascist undertones, meshing workers' rights with nationalism. Perón's efforts at nationalizing Argentine industry were apparent during his first two years as president (1946–48), and by the end of 1948 his government became a dictatorship. Many of the crimes committed during Argentina's Dirty War saw their origins during this dark era of Perón's rule.

Bortnik's portrayal of consumerism is a world of mounting disillusion and fragmentation of community, wounds of a tyrannical industrialized vision sowed by Perón that have isolated the individual. Bruno Bettelheim, in *The Informed Heart*, warns us of the addiction to market-driven economies that foment consumerism to the point of replacing the search for emotional contentment with material goods: "The greatest danger of our machine made wealth grows out of this: that for the first time we are living in an age when material comfort is possible for almost everyone. But if this, because it is so much more available, is sought not in addition to emotional contentment but in lieu of it, then there is a danger of becoming addicted to it" (62–63). Bortnik's stories "Socorro" (Help) and "El último día" (The Final Day) are a culmination of the desperation and disenchantment accumulating in a world where individuals do not understand their place or function in society—a society overwrought with intolerance, imposed structures, and bureaucracy leading to personal crises. These stories scream in opposition to restraints and regulations, in opposition to the "machine." "Socorro" is literally a list of rules, laws, and bureaucratic regulations that put limits on individuals' rights. After a list of approximately one hundred and fifty limitations, the piece shouts "¡¡Socorro!!" [Help!]

"El último día" is a parody and a tragedy. The central character of the story is led to an existential crisis. Her life is inundated with propaganda, beauty products, diet products, things that she must do because they will supposedly make her more beautiful and happy. In a sense, she is Ani-Nú trying to perform her prescribed identity contrary to her own nature. The woman of "El último día" is conscious that none of these devices has given her the slightest bit of satisfaction, her life is empty, and she sees suicide as her only option to put an end to the vicious cycle in which she is tangled. It is, evidently, a gloomier end than Ani-Nú's.

Bortnik exposes the failure of consumerism by listing the negative qualities of these products, which are so attractively advertised and packaged but completely impractical:

Se calzó las chinelas de andar anatómico con aire fatigado. . . . El cepillo especialmente diseñado para ser implacable, se rompió mientras se frotaba los dientes con la pasta que huele como si su boca solo masticara flores. . . . Se lavó la cabeza con el champú que restaura y vitaminiza cada pelo, pero descrubrió que irritaba los ojos. (33)

She put on her anatomically designed slippers and walked with an air of fatigue. . . . The especially designed toothbrush that left you plaque-free broke while she brushed her teeth with toothpaste that smelled as though she only ate flowers. . . . She washed her hair with shampoo that restores the nutrients to each hair, but she discovered that it irritates her eyes.

Bortnik's satirical tone in this story calls to mind Rosario Castellanos' play *El eterno femenino* (1975), in which a beauty parlor is equipped with hair dryers that induce women to have a variety of dreams. The play is the quintessential parody of the preexisting myths of women's identity and exposes the farce of society's concepts of "beauty" and "happiness." The dystopic world in which the protagonist of "El último día" lives is inundated with superficiality and devoid of community, solidarity, and individuality. The emphasis placed on buying the right products and eating the right foods in order to achieve happiness has left the protagonist utterly alone.

Her inability to continue coping with the solitude and her meaningless daily rituals drives her to end her life:

Antes de cerrar la puerta miró el departamento y pensó que, desarreglado y todo, igual parecía la casa de alguien que no vivía allí. . . . Por la fuerza de la

costumbre se deslizó hacia su escritorio con el andar de pantera aprendido
en solo diez lecciones. Pero, como siempre, nadie la miró. Desenfundó la
máquina que hace todo por usted, menos descansar y trabajó acunada por la
música que funciona, para que no funcione su cerebro. . . . Se sentó en un
bar y tomó un trago de la bebida que sólo toman los que pueden. Cuando
pidió la segunda copa pensó que, con esa, ya había ingerido el equivalente a
las calorías ahorradas pacientemente a lo largo del día. Se tiró de cabeza al
río en el mismo momento en que se encendían todos los avisos luminosos.

Before closing the door she looked around the apartment and thought,
messy and everything, it still seemed like a home no one lived in. . . . Out of
habit she slid toward her desk with a panther's gait that she learned in only
ten lessons. But, as always, no one looked at her. She uncovered the machine
that does everything for you except rest and she worked lulled by the music
that works so that your brain won't. . . . She sat at a bar and downed a shot
of the drink that only those who can drink order. When she asked for
another round she thought that she had already ingested all the calories she
had patiently saved throughout the day. She dove head first into the river
just as the billboards were lighting up.

The protagonist, perhaps a writer, cannot even think for herself. This
story is an emphatic critique of the consumption driven by capitalist
ventures in which value is placed on productivity and consumption, and
individuals become just another cog in the corporate machine. In her
misery, conscious of her meaningless role in such a world, she commits
suicide at the end of the day. Evidently, "El último día" may be read as
the struggle of an artist whose creativity is suffocated by the veil of censorship enforced by the dictatorship.

This harsh critique of materially driven culture and capitalism plays
out in "Ene la Perfecta" (Ene the Perfect) with a list of over one hundred things humans have created and decided to preserve, excluding
plants and animals. Bortnik proposes a pessimistic end to human existence, faulting the egoism and greed fomented by capitalism. "Capaz
de tanta basura y tanta maravilla" (17) [Capable of so much trash and
so many marvels], humans are responsible for their own destruction.

"Juguemos en el bosque" (Let's Play in the Woods) further portrays
humans' naiveté and ignorance regarding the consequences of their
actions. Set in an imaginary world, a forest, is a sheltered world in which
the *lobo*, the wolf, is seemingly distant. In the forest, the *criaturas*, the
young animals, play at competitive games fomenting personal achieve-
ment, greed, and the trimmings pertinent to a consumer society. Never

questioning the inherent consequences of these games and never fully satisfied with their achievements, they decide to face their greatest fear and challenge the wolf, who is rumored to lurk somewhere in the forest. This fatal decision ends the story, alluding to the wolf's appearance and the "end of the game"—the death of the *criaturas* who thought there was no limit to their utopia. "Juguemos en el bosque" serves as allegory for a disenchanted world where one is never protected from the danger suggested by Bettelheim, and from capitalist ventures that eventually lead to the destruction portrayed in "Ene la Perfecta," devoid of life.

Published in the same period, Bortnik's "Mi tío Lito" (My Uncle Lito) offers the same message through social realism. The story portrays the disenchantment of a hard-working socialist-minded Uncle Lito, who works all his life with the objective of offering his children a better life and a better world. His lifelong efforts, however, have not achieved his goals:

> Ahora sin embargo, se avergüenza de otras cosas: de creer todavía lo que creía, a pesar de que su trabajo ya no es una manera de respirar, sino una forma de ahogarse. De sentir todavía lo que siente, a pesar de que sus sentimientos no bastan para proteger a su familia. (19)

> Now, however, he's ashamed of other things: of still believing what he did, even though his work is no longer a breath of fresh air but suffocating; of still feeling what he does, even though his feelings cannot protect his family.

Bortnik then inserts herself and the reader in the very world that has so disappointed Uncle Lito in the final line of the story: "Y ahora él, ustedes y yo vivimos en un mundo que ha conseguido hacerlo llorar de impotencia" [And now he, all of you, and I live in a world that has succeeded in making him cry out of helplessness]. She thereby imposes disenchantment on her readers and shares the responsibility of this failing world with them.

Bettelheim calls this reality an "imbalance," when the modern external progress grows to such a degree that humans seem to be left behind, unable to achieve emotional integration: "The challenge of repeated choices as to which of many unsuitable jobs to select, which of several imperfect party platforms to support, which of many tempting but often not too essential gadgets to buy, confronts the modern citizen with his own lack of decision. Rarely do these choices really satisfy his deepest needs. Therefore, the psychic energy spent in reaching a decision is wasted and the individual feels drained of energy without purpose" (79–80). The world of labor in modern times and that of one's deeper spiritual needs do not match. Thus, the author in ¡¡Socorro!!, the woman of "El ultimo día," and Tío Lito suffer immense frustration and disenchantment, which lead to existential crises.

Violence and Memory

The stories that follow carry over a sense of disenchantment and crisis. They are riddled with losses and begin to incorporate elliptical spaces that provide opportunities for the performance of mourning. The recurring ellipses in "Crecé tranquilo" (Grow Calmly) and "¿Te acordás?" (Do You Remember?) are breaks in narration where both the narrator and the reader are haunted by loss and initiate a nostalgic journey into memory work. In "El baúl" (The Trunk), photos are the symbolic tomb of the disappeared, a theme that will reappear later in "Cuatro fotos."

In "Crecé tranquilo," an elderly man sits fatigued on a bench and begins a journey through memory. First, he wonders about the fountain of youth he had envisioned as a child, which would someday shield him from old age. Then he recalls his loved ones: first his mother, then Marina (perhaps his wife), and then his oldest son. They all seem to have died. The elderly man is plagued by recurring memories and has particular difficulty facing the recollection of his oldest son:

> Después se acordó de su hijo mayor. Abrió los ojos. ¿Por qué estaba allí ese recuerdo? No era su turno. Intentó volver al diario. Su hijo mayor se parecía al abuelo pensó, como siempre, se reía contagioso y todas las mañanas tenía ganas de cantar. Si viviera . . . otra sería la vida. (31)

> And then he remembered his oldest son. He opened his eyes. Why was that memory there? It wasn't his turn. He tried to read the newspaper. His oldest son looked like his grandfather, he thought as always: he laughed contagiously and he always yearned to sing in the mornings. If he were alive . . . life would be different.

His son's death is unresolved, and therefore, his memory is haunting. The father is perennially unprepared to accept his son's unexpected death and wishes it had never happened. The narration suggests that life would be different had he not died, implying that life would be different for everyone were there no Dirty War and that life would be different for all of those whose children have been killed. The ellipsis following "Si viviera . . ." allows memory work and potential mourning to take place. Silence and absence resound in this elliptical space, which releases a polyphony of images and possibilities: his son's laughter, his singing, what life might be like if he were still alive. This technique, which Bortnik uses in subsequent stories, stimulates the reader's imagination.[15]

Shortly after this meditation, he watches a young couple kissing nearby. His gaze is stifled as the young man sees him and raises his arm toward him in a Nazi-like gesture, forcing the man to look away and berate himself for ever having stared. He continues seated on the bench and a young child playing nearby asks him whether being old is unpleasant. The elderly man does not respond right away. His initial instinct is to answer truthfully and admit his unhappiness, but he changes his mind and simply tells the boy, "crecé tranquilo" [grow up calmly]. This story exposes the desire to protect future generations from the atrocities of the Dirty War, but evidently, the story's title is ironic in a world burdened with fascist tendencies, violence, and haunting absence. Later, in discussing Gambaro's "Buscando la compañía del árbol" (Seeking the Tree's Company), I address the issue of the *transgenerational phantom*, proposed by Nicholas Abraham, whereby silence does not serve to protect but unconsciously passes trauma on to future generations.

The repercussions of repressing the truth are seen in the story published one month later, "¿Te acordás?," the first of Bortnik's stories to deal explicitly with the issue of memory. The interrogative title sets the tone for memory work, and the opening paragraph begins with a definition of nostalgia and melancholy:

> Nostalgia: (del griego nostos: regreso; y algos: dolor). Tristeza causada por la ausencia de la patria, o de deudos y amigos. (Sinón. V. Melancolía) / Pesar que causa el recuerdo de algún bien perdido. (15)

> Nostalgia: (from the Greek *nostos:* return; and *algos:* pain). Sadness caused by the absence of the homeland, or relatives and friends. (Syn. Melancholy) A burden that results in the memory of something lost.

In Kafkaesque fashion, the protagonist awakens to a changed world. Everything seems to have disappeared and the narrator questions the protagonist's resistance: "a lo mejor se había quedado inmóvil mientras todo lo demás se deslizaba . . ." [maybe he had remained frozen while everything else slipped away . . .]. Here, Bortnik inserts an elliptical space, one that allows readers to think of how the world has changed, to question their own effort to challenge the disappearance, to become nostalgic for a past that is no longer, and to grow melancholy for the losses that cannot be retrieved. The narrative then brings this spiraling thought cycle to a halt and insists, "No," reminding the reader that buildings and objects still remain, an almost identical language is spoken, and similar gestures are still practiced. Nevertheless, the protagonist screams, "¿dónde está todo?" [where is everything?], only to feel ashamed by his question when he realizes that everyone else is trying to pretend that nothing at all has changed and people are the same as before.

He tries to follow suit, but unsuccessfully. His dreams are disturbing. He dreams about the Marx brothers, the episode in which Harpo is leaning against a wall, and Chico jokes, "¿estás sosteniendo el edificio?" [are you holding up the building?] and pulls Harpo away as the building crashes down. The narration repeats here three times, "El edificio se desploma" [The building is collapsing], and the protagonist becomes obsessed with compensating for the melancholy he feels. He begins, symbolically, to hold up the world around him to prevent the absence and losses from overwhelming him. Finally, he tires and realizes that he can no longer protect himself from the crypt he once worked so hard to contain, for otherwise, his missing friends and loved ones will be nothing but ghosts, and "[u]na memoria negada no alimentaba más que un ideal muerto." [a memory denied didn't feed anything but a dead ideal]. He wakes from his denial and asks the first person he sees whether he remembers him: "¿te acordás de mí?"[do you remember me?]. He is asked in return: "¿te acordás de vos?"[do you remember yourself?], implying the need to restore one's own identity, to stop living in fear. The two embrace and the world around them takes on meaning once again: "Lloraron en un abrazo. Y a medida que recordaban, el mundo comenzaba a espesarse, a rellenarse, a solidificarse." [They cried in an embrace. And while they remembered the world began to take shape and solidify.] Undoubtedly, Bortnik equates memory with healing and identity.

Loss and the preservation of memory are also central themes in "El baúl," published in February 1982. The protagonists are an older couple who perform the monthly rituals of sending letters to their daughter, who lives in another country, and going to the cemetery to visit their son's tomb. Read in the context of the Dirty War, the story immediately raises the issues of the disappeared and the exiled. The couple has a trunk full of photographs that they look through every night. Though some of them are photos of vacations and parties, happy moments, others have been inherited from "mother and grandmothers, solemn and melancholy people" and evoke loss and mourning. The trunk embodies a tomb that the couple has filled and revisits daily, symbolizing the ever-present haunting of death and the constant ritual of mourning and memory work transcending the individual. The couple mourns for others' losses as well as their own, asserting that these deaths affect a community. Their collective mourning ritual speaks to LaCapra's assessment that the "hauntingly possessive ghosts of traumatic events are not fully owned by anyone, they affect everyone" (2001 xi).

The couple hires a young man to paint their home and are especially taken with his quiet and friendly demeanor. They had planned to invent other jobs for him once he finished painting so that he could stay around and therefore cultivate for him and for them, an illusion of family. But he never finishes painting. He believes the trunk to be full of valuables and he murders the couple in order to steal its contents. Upset not to find anything but photos and some broken watches that the old man was repairing, he sets all of the pictures ablaze, once again stripping the victims of their identity and acting out the violence and erasure of memory imposed by the military regime.

The escalation of violence and fear is central to the story "Basta" (Enough), which is written in six sections that trace the events of one day in the protagonist's life. The protagonist is awakened at six-thirty in the morning by sirens in front of his apartment and can not believe that anyone would break into an apartment in such a poor neighborhood. He is also poor and feels guilty drinking coffee when it is so expensive. The electricity has gone out again, and there is no sense in wasting money on the newspaper because "las pocas cosas que se pueden creer te amargan el día" [the few believable things will ruin your day] (26). As do many of Bortnik's stories, this one speaks directly to the reader at times by using the informal *you* address. Otherwise, it is narrated in the third-person singular and guides the reader through the protagonist's day. On his way to work he crosses the street to find out what had happened but does not give the reader narrative satisfaction by revealing any information other than mentioning that the kiosk vendor out in front of the building was crying.

At seven-thirty, while on the bus, he watches a young boy nodding off to sleep and gripping the hand rail. The boy tells his friends that he and his family were searching through garbage outside the supermarket at four in the morning for food. At ten o'clock there is talk of a strike at work and general fear of the consequences. At twelve-thirty, while he is eating lunch, a little girl approaches him, begging for money, and the protagonist loses his appetite. At nine-thirty in the evening he witnesses a hold-up and a robbery by three young men with makeshift weapons, including a fake gun. The victim cries out that she had just been paid and that her husband had been mugged just two weeks ago. She insists that all thieves should be killed. When the protagonist finally turns out the lights after this full day, he looks out the window at the apartment building that was the site of so much activity earlier that morning. He recalls the older couple who lived there—how they met while singing in a choir—and finally he allows himself to cry as he thinks of the older couple opening the gas switch and taking their own lives. While ultimately giving the reader the narrative satisfaction of knowing what had happened across the street in the morning, the narration also unsettles the reader. The story ends: "Y por todos los que tienen miedo y desesperación. Y por la cara que se había visto en el espejo del baño. Y entonces se dio cuenta de que para el había llegado al momento de decir basta" [And to all those who are afraid and feel desperate. And because of the face he had seen in the bathroom mirror. And then he realized that the moment had come to say enough] and impells the reader also to say, "Enough" alongside the protagonist.

Told in the third person, "Basta" situates the reader as a spectator: hearing the sirens, seeing the poor boy on the bus and imagining his sifting through garbage in the middle of the night, watching the little girl begging for money in the pizzeria, hearing the talk of the strike and feeling the tension and vulnerability, witnessing the assault, and finally looking out the window to feel regret for the older couple who could no longer stand it. "Basta" serves as a bridge between the theme of violence and the need for empowerment and nonviolent activism, which are prevalent themes in the stories to follow. "Basta" states emphatically, "Enough," and asks how to confront this miserable and desperate reality.

Empowerment

In "Buscando" (Searching) and "El corazón de Celeste" (Celeste's Heart), published a month apart, Bortnik sets the tone for activism and protest against the dictatorial regime. She creates a man and a young girl in complete opposition to the earlier protagonists of "Tomás el ortodóxo" and "Ella y los hombres."

Unlike Tomás, who never questioned anything and was the Lord's only failure, the protagonist of "Buscando" is always curious, an insatiable explorer, always searching for different answers, different feelings, and different perspectives. He reads avidly and takes interest in everything and everyone, he ages without realizing it, and when he dies, his eyes are still open, his arms still extended, and his hands still moving as if he were searching for another life. This story marks a change in tone in Bortnik's series of short stories, moving from the themes of violence and memory to those of empowerment and nonviolence, and is followed by "El corazón de Celeste."

Similar to the protagonist of "Buscando," Celeste is a young girl who questions and takes a stand against authoritarianism. Celeste's schoolteacher represents dictatorial rule and is referred to as Maestra, Teacher, always nameless and written with a capital M. Celeste takes an oppositional and unsettling position in relation to the authority figure who is a female teacher in an all-girls' school. Rather than obeying the Maestra, who punishes the young girls by making them stand in line with their arms stretched out, Celeste challenges her by not raising her arm. The Maestra responds to Celeste's resistance by insisting once again that she do what she is told. Celeste's silent protest soon becomes vocal and she stands up to the Maestra: "Le dijo que el brazo dolía, después. Y que todos tenían frío y miedo. Y que uno no iba a la escuela para sentir dolor, frío y miedo" (13). [She told her that her arm hurt afterwards. And that all the girls were cold and afraid. And that no one went to school to feel pain, cold, and fear.] By repeatedly referring to the Maestra as a nameless authority, this story questions the institution of education in general—the instructional methods and disciplinary actions that foster an environment of obedience, complicity, and fear, not unlike the methods practiced by the dictatorial regime.

"El corazón de Celeste" works to show that one person's actions can have an impact on many. After Celeste stands up to the Maestra, almost all of her classmates also lower their arms: "el mundo mejoró después de aquél día. Y casi todas empezaron a bajar los brazos" [the world improved after that day. And almost everyone began to lower their arms]. This story glorifies Celeste's stand and further exemplifies her as a role model. Doing something significant makes her heart grow and the positive sensation makes her long to live a life committed to social and moral responsibility:

Esa noche Celeste casi no durmió, porque tenía una sensación muy extraña en el cuerpo. Una sensación que había comenzado cuando no levantó el brazo, en medio de la fila. . . . El corazón crece cuando uno hace algo que no había hecho nunca, cuando aprende algo que no sabía, cuando uno siente algo distinto y mejor, por primera vez. Y la sensación le pareció buena. Y se prometió a sí misma que su corazón seguirá creciendo y creciendo y creciendo.

That night Celeste almost didn't sleep because her body felt strange inside. A feeling had begun when she didn't raise her hand in the middle of the line, the feeling that something was growing inside her chest. It burned a little, but it didn't hurt. And she thought that if someone's legs and arms and all that, could grow, then everything inside had to grow as well. But legs and arms grow without anyone noticing, equally and gradually. The heart must grow in spurts. And it made sense to her: the heart grows when you do something you've never done before, when you learn something new, when you feel something different and better, for the first time. And the strange feeling seemed good. And she promised herself that her heart would continue growing and growing and growing.

While echoing Gandhi's belief that the highest form of spiritual freedom must be sought in the strength of the heart, Bortnik undoubtedly works to empower Argentines to strengthen their own hearts and stand up against the dictatorship that has held them silent in fear.[16]

Nonviolence

After the publication of "Basta," Bortnik's stories become increasingly concerned with ways to respond to authoritarianism, corruption, and violence without committing the same crimes; without repeating violent tactics in revenge and therefore contributing to further oppression. This is emphatically stated in the following stories, which work to encourage nonviolence and compassion: "Diferencia" (Difference), "Oferta" (Offer), "Hagamos una lista" (Let's Make a List), and "Julio Montaña Dorada" (Julio Golden Mountain).

The subject of "Diferencia" is *La Familia*, the Family, representing the Argentines in general who are held imprisoned both physically and spiritually. The story begins: "La Familia estaba prisionera. Física y espiritualmente prisionera" (17). [The Family was imprisoned. Physically and spiritually imprisoned]. The narration portrays an oppressive environment in which children do not have enough to eat and have lost their interest in everything while parents work at senseless jobs and the elderly are ill because of indifference and isolation. Significantly, "Diferencia" works to show that everyone is affected by the imprisonment and no one is untouchable. Every generation is prisoner and no one really understands why. For the prison guards, the mere fact that the Family is imprisoned is evidence that they are criminals, and no one questions the alleged crimes.

The narration carries the reader through various stages of the Family's resistance and the danger that their desperation and anger could transform the Family into "eficacísimos cómplices de muros, armas, o carceleros adiestrados" [effective accomplices of walls, weapons, or adept jailers]. "Diferencia" effectively emphasizes the thin line that distinguishes victim from victimizer. The only liberation from the vulnerability this victim/victimizer binary imposes is through fortification of one's spiritual energy, which can transform the melancholic and nostalgic memory of freedom into a motivating force devoid of vengeance. After much time and patience, the Family gains "mucha energía espiritual para enseñar a los niños a aprender de ellos, la imaginación y el valor, la multiplicidad de ideas y el respeto por lo distinto, la solidaridad y la ternura, la dignidad y la tolerancia" [a lot of spiritual energy to teach their children about imagination, self-worth, diversity of opinions and respect for that which is different, solidarity and tenderness, dignity and tolerance]. Dedication to fomenting this spiritual energy eventually leads the Family to their spiritual freedom, which consequently liberates them physically as well: "la Familia se dedicó, sin descanso, a destruir la prisión y todos sus mecanismos. Hasta que ni un sola piedra, ni una sola arma cuestionaran su liberación" [the Family was dedicated, tirelessly, to destroying the prison and all its mechanisms. Until not a stone, not even one weapon could question its freedom]. Even the prison guards grow envious of the Family's strength and freedom abounding with tolerance, solidarity, and compassion.

The dialogue at the story's end transforms the reader's position into one of active presence. The guards speak to the Family in the third-person-plural *ustedes* (you) form, implying that the reader too is a member of the Family: "¿De qué les ha servido recuperar su libertad? Ahora que han destruido todos los instrumentos del poder, ¿cómo harán prevalecer su causa sobre la nuestra? ¿Cómo nos someterán?" [What use was regaining your freedom? Now that you've destroyed all the means of power, how will your mission prevail over ours? How will you subdue us?] The Family, and the reader, respond collectively, "Si empleáramos los mismos métodos, ¿dónde estaría la diferencia?" [If we use the same methods, how are we any different from you?] Here, the narrative emphasizes the importance of not creating the same power structures as the victimizers, the value of creativity and solidarity —accepting others, fomenting spiritual energy and tolerance. Otherwise, the survivors of oppression would be no different from their torturers.

In "Oferta" and "Hagamos la lista" Bortnik literally works further to sell this idea of cultivating spirituality, creativity, imagination, and one's own freedom from the oppressive reality. The contagious power of one to affect its parts as in "El corazón de Celeste" and the spirituality encouraged in "Diferencia" find their way into the heart of Buenos Aires, into the subway where seeds of hope are sown beneath the urban polis. During moments of national economic crisis, the Buenos Aires subway is especially rife with vendors, musicians, and dancers working from car to car hoping to make some money. Often, the vendors sell pens, key chains, notebooks, breath mints, batteries, and other miscellaneous items. The vendor in these two stories, however, offers ideas, invaluable ideas to help passengers live in a world of negativity and violence without succumbing to it.

The salesman of "Oferta" offers the passengers something that has cost him dearly, "excesivamente caro," and asks them to place their own price on it. The passengers listen apprehensively at first as he tells them:

Les ofrezco una idea. No está completa, no puedo afirmar que sea original, no puedo asegurar que funcione igual para todos. Pero sé que es una buena idea. Porque antes de ofrecerla a los señores pasajeros la he probado yo mismo. (52)

I offer you an idea. It's not complete, I can't assure that it's original, and I can't promise that it'll work the same for all. But I know that it's a good idea. Because before offering it to passengers I myself have tested it out.

Once again, the use of the third-person plural, *ustedes*, invites the reader into the subway car, to hear the vendor's sales pitch. He tells the passengers that everyone is free, "todos nosotros somos libres," provoking some laughter and agitation among the passengers and probably among the readers as well. He continues regardless and says:

Aunque no tengamos trabajo, aunque la que ganemos no alcance, aunque nunca podamos recuperar lo que estamos perdiendo desde hace tantos años, aunque tengamos que soportar que se nos repitan mentiras viejas como si fueran mentiras nuevas, aunque nos dé indignación y vergüenza por nosotros y por nuestros hijos, aunque no podamos ni imaginarnos cómo sería vivir sin represión y sin miedo, señoras y señores pasajeros, hay una parte en cada uno de ustedes, un pedacito, adentro en la cabeza, en el pecho o, a veces, cuando duele, en el estomago, un pedacito en todos y cada uno de nosotros, que es libre. Permítanme un ejemplo: nadie los ha obligado a escucharme. Nadie les ha impedido insultarme. Nada nos obliga a maltratarnos, nada nos impide intentar ayudarnos. Quiero decir, señoras y señores pasajeros: podemos elegir libremente casi una sola cosa, a estas alturas: vivir como hombres o como bestias acorraladas.

Even though we're out of work, even though our earnings aren't enough, even though we can't recuperate what we've been losing for so many years, even though we have to put up with them repeating old lies as if they were new ones, even though it angers and shames us as well as our children, even though we cannot even imagine what life would be like without repression and fear, ladies and gentleman passengers, there is a part of each one of us, a small piece, in our minds, in our hearts or, sometimes, when it hurts, in our guts, a small piece in each and everyone of us, that is free. Allow me to give you an example: no one has forced you to listen to me. No one has kept you from insulting me. Nothing forces us to mistreat ourselves, nothing keeps us from trying to help ourselves. What I'm trying to say, ladies and gentlemen passengers: we can freely choose almost only one thing, at this stage: to live as human beings and not as caged animals.

In response, the passengers, listeners, or perhaps even the Familia, freely choose to pay the salesman for his idea. Though Bortnik does imply the importance of standing up for oneself, questioning, and taking responsibility for the world in previous stories, the vendor's voice is the most direct and rhetorical of all the published stories prior to September 1982. It is here where Bortnik narrates as a motivational speaker and works most emphatically to empower her readers to keep believing in themselves and in the potential for a better future even though, as the vendor affirms, it is almost impossible to do so when one lives in a constant state of crisis. The vendor, or spiritual guru, or perhaps even Bortnik herself works to lift the spirits from below and from within, thereby to address the internal wounds of the nation. The subterranean salesman represents this need to work from the bottom up, from the inside out, to encourage individuals to be introspective and search out that space that has been hidden away and claim it as one's own in order to protect oneself from the oppression imposed externally, symbolically from above.

For even in the *lager* of Auschwitz, where one could not imagine feeling any more helpless, Primo Levi emphasizes the importance of not giving up one's own sense of self even though all seems virtually lost in the deliberate demolition of humanity:

> Precisely because the Lager was a great machine to reduce us to beasts, we must not become beasts; that even in this place one can survive, and therefore one must want to survive, to tell the story, to bear witness; and that to survive we must force ourselves to save at least the skeleton, the scaffolding, the form of civilization. We are slaves, deprived of every right, exposed to every insult, condemned to certain death, but we still possess one power, and we must defend it with all our strength for it is the last—the power to refuse our consent. So we must certainly wash our faces without soap in dirty water and dry ourselves on our jackets. We must polish our shoes, not because the regulation states it, but for dignity and propriety. We must walk erect, without dragging our feet, not in homage to Prussian discipline but to remain alive, not to begin to die. (41)

The subway vendor appears again in July 1983, almost ten months later, in the story "Hagamos una lista." He is tired but continues working. Again, he offers an idea, and he repeats the preamble of "Oferta":

> Les ofrezco una idea. No está completa, no puedo afirmar que sea original, no puedo asegurar que funcione de la misma manera para todos. . . . Pero sé que es una buena idea. Porque antes de ofrecerlas a los señores pasajeros la he probado yo mismo. (20)

> I offer you an idea. It's not complete, I can't assure that it's original, and I can't promise that it'll work the same for all. But I know that it's a good idea. Because before offering it to passengers I myself have tested it out.

He reminds the passengers and the readers of the violent images and murder stories they are constantly exposed to in the daily media—the sinister reminder of the oppressive society that threatens their lives. Though the papers will not stop publishing stories of violence, he stresses the importance that everyone believe that not everything is lost. He motivates passengers, and the readers of *HUM®*, to look inward and seek an interior space where they can retain a positive perspective and preserve hope. He proposes that all of them make a personal list of positive things, images, and people in their lives in order to combat all of the negativity and violence. He then reads his own list to the passengers. It is full of compassionate and humanitarian gestures of everyday life:

Mi primo Tito, que es médico porque le gusta curar a la gente y que tiene úlcera porque traga todo el dolor que no puede aliviar; los señores Álvarez, Martín y Barbeito y la señorita Nélida, que venden máquinas de escribir en frente de mi casa y tratan a todo el mundo como a un semejante; el dueño del garage que hace favores como si viviera de eso y el Morocho que lava los coches mientras da consejos que parecen abrazos; el cartero que entrega las cartas con dirección equivocada porque se siente responsable de que la comunicación no se interrumpa; mi abuela con nombre de flor, que enterró a sus hijos y siguió siendo capaz de querer a los hijos de otros. . . . (20)

My Uncle Tito, who is a doctor because he enjoys healing people and who has an ulcer because he internalizes all the pain he cannot relieve; the Alvarez', Martín and Barbeito and Ms. Nélida, who sell typewriters in front of my house and trat everyone as equals; the garage boss who does favors as if it's his job and the guy who washes cars while giving advice that seem like hugs; the postman who delivers letters with the wrong address because he feels personally responsible that people don't lose touch; my grandmother with the name of a flower, who buried her own children and is still capable of loving other people's children. . . .

While some of the passengers search for money, others pay him by making their own lists. Similarly to "Diferencia" and "Oferta," it emphasizes the importance of self-preservation and empowerment, which must originate within, and it promotes inner peace and spirituality as stepping stones for effecting external change. Most compelling is the mention of the grandmother who buried her own children, the vendor's own parents, and continues to care for the children of others.

The second to last story Bortnik published in *HUM®* features Julio Montaña Dorada, an empowered survivor of an Austrian Jewish family all but vanished by "pogroms, revoluciones, invasiones, y reconquistas, guerras locales y mundiales, soluciones finales y purificación de minorías" (17) [pogroms, revolutions, invasions, conquests, local and world wars, final solutions, as well as ethnic cleansing]. His once numerous family is all but a memory: "Aquella interminable cadena de los Montaña Dorada, aquella infinita trama de amor y fatigas, recuerdos, peleas, y celebraciones, desapareció de la faz de la Tierra" [That endless chain of the Montaña Dorada family, that infinite web of loves and fatigues, memories, arguments and celebrations, disappeared from the face of the Earth]. Julio is left orphaned and immigrates to Buenos Aires. As a prime example of working through trauma and transforming one's suffering into collective empowerment, Julio works as a guard in an orphanage, where he symbolically forms a new family, one made up of others who have been victims of the course of history. Although he never has biological children of his own, he eventually runs the orphanage himself, and it grows from a small home into a village.

The story ends, emphasizing the everlasting repercussions of nonviolence and compassion:

> Julio Montaña Dorada, el único sobreviviente de aquella interminable cadena, ha sembrado el mundo de una semilla indestructible. Ninguno de los niños a los que dio amor lleva su nombre. Pero entre todos forman una cordillera demasiado alta y demasiado extensa para que cualquier odio pueda volver a borrar su familia de la faz de la Tierra. (17)

> Julio Montaña Dorada, the only survivor of that infinite chain, has planted an indestructible seed in the world. None of the children he loved bears his name. But altogether they form a mountain chain too tall and too wide for any form of hatred to ever erase his family from the face of the Earth again.

Rather than perpetuate the hatred that decimated his family and sent him into exile, Julio Montaña Dorada practices nonviolence and shares his love with others who suffer, a gesture that has manifold positive repercussions. Though seemingly utopic scenarios, these stories in their tone and momentum ring with Mahatma Gandhi's theory of nonviolent resistance. Gandhi pledged that one could not counter violence with violence, but rather, one must work to resist violence and constantly work to overcome it by viewing the sin of the aggressor as an opportunity to generate compassion.[17] Nonviolence is not passive resistance, but it is the willingness to die for truth, to suffer without retaliation, to love so-called enemies because, Gandhi states, "For a non-violent person the whole world is one family. He will thus fear none, nor will others fear him" (67). Bortnik's use of the term *Familia* to describe the prisoners of "Diferencia" seems more than coincidental. Though imprisoned, they did not resolve to be prisoners. Their freedom is achieved through their mental state, whose strength inspires the weaker prison guards to question their own position as oppressors.

"Cuatro fotos"

The final story of the collection, the thirtieth, is entitled "Cuatro fotos" (Four Photos) and appears in *HUM®* number 112, of September 1983.

Bortnik returns to the importance of memory emphatically pro-
nounced in "Dieciocho años," the hauntingly possessive ghosts of "¿Te
acordás?" and "Crecé tranquilo," and the symbolic tombs—the photographs—of "El baúl." "Cuatro fotos" returns to the site of memory and
mourning.

The narrator describes four photographs, the only traces left of a
young couple she once knew, perhaps her own children. Each photo
carries a story, a memory that the narrator recalls about a couple who
had met as children: a nameless young woman referred to as Ella (She)
and Braulio. The inability to name the woman marks the narrator's
resistance to accepting that Ella has disappeared. The couple fell in
love, married, were building a home, and were taken away by the Triple
A. The four photographs are the only material evidence of their lives:
everything else has "disappeared." This is a story about absence. It is
full of ellipses and the reader is left to fill in the missing history. The
ellipses serve as a textual presence for that which is no longer and creates a space for the resuscitation of memory and nostalgia for the past.
The repetition of the ellipses throughout the story is the repetition of
fragmentation itself: the recurrence of the open wounds haunting the
narrator. Within the ellipses lies a truth that cannot yet be articulated.
They are the fissure that separates loss and language, the fits and starts
of initiating mourning work after a traumatic experience.

The reader is driven to fill in those spaces and potentially participate
in the process of mourning and feeling his/her own losses. The palpable trauma of the woman holding the four photos and telling the love
story of the missing couple is unsettling to the reader, who is now posi-
tioned as witness and listener. The narrator cherishes these photos as a
lifeline to a much happier past. Similarly to "El baúl," the photos have
become a symbolic tomb. She establishes a dialogue through these
remains, the only physical site of mourning in which she can resuscitate the couple. The final lines of the story are "Nada quedó. Nada.
Estas cuatro fotos, solamente. Es lo único que hay de ellos dos. Y nuestra memoria" [Nothing remained. Nothing. Only these four photos.
This is all that's left of the two of them. And our memory] (11). Again,
the first-person plural, *nuestra* (our), indicates the reader's responsibility to honor the dead and remember the disappeared.

In Marianne Hirsch's *Family Frames*, she studies the relationship to
photographs of the deceased: "It is precisely the indexical nature of the
photo, its status as relic, or trace, or fetish—its 'direct' connection with
the material presence of the photographed person—that at once inten-

sifies its status as harbinger of death and, at the same time and con-comitantly, its capacity to signify life" (20). These photos of Braulio and Ella now mark their death, their "having [once] been there" before the camera, before the eyes of their family and friends. Now these photos are markers of their absence and they are a harbinger of death and catastrophe, visual reminders of lives on the verge of ending. The "direct" connection with the photographed person is now the direct connection with the dead person. The photos, in the sense that they incite the process of narration, become dynamic sites for the perfor-mativity of mourning. As proposed by J. L. Austin, it is the utterance of the word that is *the* initiating incident in the performance of the act.[18] The photos aid in the extraction of the utterance.

In the film *La historia oficial*, "Cuatro fotos" is reproduced in a café where Sarah and Alicia meet to discover that Alicia's adopted daughter may indeed be Sarah's missing granddaughter, born in a clandestine prison. The original short story is modified in the film to imply that Sarah's daughter was pregnant when she was taken by the Triple A. Thus, while denouncing the theft and traficking of babies, the story transforms into a space for hope of potential life directly connected with Sarah's daughter, who was most likely killed after giving birth in prison. Sarah insists that her granddaughter was born while her daugh-ter was being held in a clandestine prison during the Dirty War, and she persists in searching for her estranged grandchild, who she believes has been given to a wealthy couple associated with the authoritarian regime, unable to have children of their own.

The meeting in the cafe takes place while Alicia is gaining awareness of what has been going on in her own country. Her husband, Roberto's, involvement in the dictatorship also unfolds before her eyes. In the film, the four photographs are no longer a site of elliptical space, absence, and mourning, but a site of apparition, of hope, and of protest. Whereas in the *cuentito* they are a departure, death, and nostalgia, the film allows a possibility of birth, an arrival, a resistance to injustice—a grandmother potentially being united with her granddaughter and therefore rescuing a living body, an active presence of her murdered children. The photos are a site of hope and reencounter with the departed. The discovery of Sarah's granddaughter also affirms the importance that the searches continue, that the circling of the Plaza de Mayo with posters of the disappeared is necessary for the discovery of truth and will have positive results.

In considering LaCapra's claim that a measure of critical distance and socially engaged memory work is essential to successful work through trauma, Sarah's activism in *La historia oficial* is a cinematic representation of successful memory work. Although still visibly plagued by her loss, Sarah has undone her entrapment enough to gain critical distance and work fervently toward social justice. The narrative published in "Cuatro fotos" coupled with the activism portrayed in *La historia oficial* is further evidence that Borntik's work transcends the private exercise of memory work to one that is more public, therefore bridging art and activism.

13. "Asesinos" ("Murderers" Graffiti on Boston Bank, Buenos Aires. July 2003). Photo by Robert M. Levine.

3

"Empathic Unsettlement" in Griselda Gambaro's *Lo mejor que se tiene*

People have lost the ability to see the facts of reality. The dead have become numbers, statistics. But if the dead are seen on stage, . . . if we see it in a theater, and we're able to "see" what death means, the war, the children, the cries, the infinite pain, then that moves us in a different way. The esthetic act has to awaken us, has to sensitize us to all the false information, the deformation of feelings and ideas upon which our society is based.

—Griselda Gambaro

GRISELDA GAMBARO (B. 1928) HAS FORGED A FUNDAMENTAL SPACE for artists to express a critical voice in Argentina. Early in her literary career, she dedicated herself to narrative but she later gained distinction through her work in theater. The staging of her production *El desatino* (1965), marked a break with traditional norms of performance in Argentina and has been representative of Gambaro's distinct work ever since. Her theater has been staged internationally and has received many prestigious awards.[1] Gambaro established herself in the theater, a genre that calls for a performative space and a spectator. Writing and directing a work for performance is equivalent to choreographing a "coming out" of sorts, which allows the theater to uncover truths and stimulate the audience's consciousness. Gambaro's influence on the audience, her readers, and fellow writers is in a sense a parallel to the influence the Madres and Abuelas of the Plaza de Mayo have had on other groups of protest that have since made their voices heard in public spaces (Memoria Activa, Los Docentes, HIJOS, Los Jubilados, etc.). The public space to which I refer is one that coincides with Habermas's concept of the *public sphere*, "a site of production and circulation of discourses that can in principle be critical of the state . . . it is not an arena of market relations, but rather one of discursive relations, a theater for debating and deliberating rather than for buying or selling" (Fraser 110–11). Indeed, the space cultivated by Gambaro, both in her theater and in her narrative, is one of deliberation, a space in which individual and collective identities are articulated and discovered, where repressed narratives are unleashed and critical of the state.

Shortly after the publication of her novel *Ganarse la muerte* (1976), Gambaro's work was censored in Argentina. She was blacklisted and went into exile during the most violent years of the dictatorship:

> Después de la prohibición de *Ganarse la muerte*, se cortaron casi todos mis accesos de comunicación con el público. No podía publicar, no se me hacían entrevistas, no podía publicar ni estrenar. . . . Y yo no soy una persona valiente, capaz de enfrentar directamente a la violencia. No he hecho más que escribir en la soledad de mi cuarto. Pero en ese momento, no tenía, ni siquiera esa soledad porque todos los espacios públicos y privados estaban invadidos por la dictadura, y yo no tenía recursos de resistencia efectiva para oponerme. En la Argentina no me sentía útil porque no podía trabajar, así que me fui a España y me quedé tres años (42).[2]

> After *Ganarse la muerte* (Earn Your Death) was banned, all my communication channels with the public were cut off. I couldn't publish, I wasn't interviewed, I could neither publish nor debut any plays. [. . .] And I'm not a courageous person, capable of directly confronting violence. I've never done naything other than write in the solitude of my room. But at that time, I didn't even have that solitude because every public and private space was invaded by the dictatorship, and I didn't have any effective weapons of resistence to fight with. I felt useless in Argentina because I couldn't work, so I left for Spain and lived there for three years.

Although censorship and danger were not threatening her in Spain, Gambaro was unable to write theater while in exile because she felt disconnected from her audience and unable to establish the dialogue that the theater demands of her: "La necesidad de escribir teatro te la da el público, ese público inmediato y cercano con el que se ha compartido la misma historia, la misma experiencia. En España yo no lo tenía. Entonces, ese lado mío permanecía inerte y silencioso." [The public gives you the need to write theater, that immediate and close public with whom one's shared the same history, the same experience. I didn't have that in Spain. So that part of me remained inert and silent.][3] She did, however, write another novel, *Dios no nos quiere contentos* (God Doesn't Want Us to Be Happy) (1979). Having experienced censorship, internal exile within Argentina, where her work was banned, and external exile upon leaving the country, where she felt disconnected from her audience and therefore unable to write theater, Gambaro is highly attentive to the issues of community and alienation many have experienced as a result of totalitarian regimes. This theme of double exile, internal and external, shows up often in her work and especially in the short stories of her latest collection, *Lo mejor que se tiene* (The Best There Is) (1998).

By producing narrative and theater that reveal the injustice of fascist regimes and the importance of memory, Gambaro has resisted the silence imposed by authoritarian discourse. While most analyses dealing with her narrative focus on her novels,[4] this chapter is devoted to showing how her short stories published in the aftermath of the Dirty War not only uncover and subvert the repression of a patriarchal discourse, but also give voice to a society that must work through a traumatic past in order to recover its identity. And, in giving "voice," these stories also reveal the crisis of expression in the aftermath of terror. Her short stories make no direct reference to the Dirty War itself but clearly represent a society that is scarred and haunted by absence and crisis.

Gambaro's theater has been described by Diana Taylor as a "theater of crisis," where she represents a violent reality in order to heighten her audience's awareness.[5] Taylor quotes Gambaro:

la gente ha perdido sensibilidad para ver los datos de la realidad. . . . Pero si eso lo vemos en el teatro, y somos capaces de *ver* lo que significa la muerte, la Guerra, los chicos, los llantos, el dolor infinito, entonces eso nos moviliza de una manera muy distinta[6]

People have lost the ability to see the facts of reality. But if we see it in a theater, and we're able to "see" what death means, the war, the children, the cries, the infinite pain, then that moves us in a different way.

And true to her words, Gambaro's plays have been noted for their violent representations of reality (e.g., *Decir sí, Información para extranjeros, El campo*). Although her short stories do not represent vivid portrayals of the physical violence of the Dirty War, I borrow Taylor's words and propose that the stories be read as examples of crisis, for they guide the reader through the haunting and isolating effects of trauma and loss. The repercussions of physical and psychological violence are represented in the rupture of language, the fragmentation of community, and the isolation of the individual. The ironic title, *Lo mejor que se tiene* (The Best There Is), pokes at the fact that Argentina, in 1998, weighed down by immense foreign debt and under "democratic" rule by a corrupt government that has granted amnesty to convicted murderers, does not have much to offer.

Lo mejor que se tiene was published after a decade of civilian rule and won the Premio de Argentina de Letras. The stories making up this collection speak to the devastating repercussions of trauma and the horrific legacy of dictatorships and fascist ideologies. I have selected five stories from this collection that are particularly emblematic of the vast representations of postdictatorial repercussions in Gambaro's repertoire: "Nosferatu," "El trastocamiento," "Buscando la compañía del árbol," "El encuentro," and "El misterio de dar." This selection embodies the traumatic symptoms and signs that resurface as a result of political pressure and cultural tendency to forget. While heavily laden with the issues of memory, trauma, and marginalization, these stories speak to the phenomenon that blindness and silence lead to an escalation of traumatic isolation of survivors of repressive events, which may inevitably lead to madness and even suicide if not inverted with discourse and compassion. How can survivors of Argentina's Dirty War accept that their torturers, criminals guilty of torturing and massacring tens of thousands of people, have been pardoned and continue to walk the streets? The Chilean author Ariel Dorfman addresses this issue directly in his play *La muerte y la doncella* (Death and the Maiden) (1991), in which a survivor of torture during Chile's Pinochet dictatorship comes face-to-face with her torturer fifteen years later. Argentina is plagued by neuroses—survivors and victims of the Dirty War can never feel "secure" in a nation where murderers are supported by the governing body. The protagonists of the stories are riddled with trauma and isolation fomented by the lack of an empathic other or an other to whom they may tell their story. These stories project an environment that is fragmented and desperately seeking solace.

Gambaro's stories, via third-person narrative, expose the tension created by the complexity of trauma—the apprehension, the inability, and the desperation to confront the trauma. As it is always conceptualized as that which is out of one's reach or that which is "unspeakable," trauma, unattended to, writhes in its silence or painful absence. An "empathic listener," however, creates a rhetorical presence that dulls the pain of the traumatized and reduces his/her solitude. In compliance with LaCapra's definition of the "secondary witness" as one who "puts [him/her] self in the other's position while recognizing the difference of that position and hence not taking the other's place," I suggest that the reader of *Lo mejor que se tiene* becomes a "secondary witness" of the trauma Gambaro unveils in her stories.[7] By the same token, the listener or "secondary witness" also partially experiences the trauma during the act of listening, as explained by Shoshana Felman and Dori Laub in *Testimony: Crises of Witnessing in Literature, Psychoanalysis, and History:* "The emergence of the narrative which is being listened to—and heard—is . . . the process and place wherein the cognizance, the 'knowing' of the event is given birth to. The listener, therefore, is a party to the creation of knowledge *de novo* . . . the listener to trauma comes to be a participant and a co-owner of the traumatic event: through his very listening, he comes to partially experience trauma in himself. . . . The listener, therefore, has to be at the same time a witness to the trauma witness and a witness to himself" (57–58). Avoiding first-person narration, eliminating the *Yo* (I), makes the reader less likely to place him/herself in the position of the victim. Furthermore, it is by positioning the reader in the act of witnessing, as the spectator of the drama, the listener and witness of trauma, that Gambaro may be said to achieve social responsibility— heightening awareness and making the individual experience a collective one. Further, as in Freud's notion of transference, the narrator and the listener to the narrative establish a dialogic relationship that fosters a transmission and a reception, thus contributing to the "communicative chain" suggested by Peter Brooks. Ultimately, Gambaro's stories change the reader and engender compassion.

My reading of *Lo mejor que se tiene* as a collection of short stories founded in "crisis" and unfinished mourning is supported by the very first entry of the collection, entitled "Nosferatu." The literary presence of the vampire, the undead who cannot be at rest, in a nation where 30,000 *desaparecidos* have never received "proper" burial rites is a likely phenomenon upon consideration of Lawrence Rickels's *The Vampire Lectures:* "The wicked or excommunicated person, the perjurer, apostate, the person who died under a curse, and the person (often the same person) who was buried without proper rites, were each in turn up for finalist entry as corpse that could not decompose or stay at rest" (4). Freud, in *Totem and Taboo*, explains that the ghosts and demons that haunted the so-called savages were indeed dead people who had not been properly mourned. The vampire, emblematic of unfinished mourning, represents the haunting presence of the disappeared lurking throughout Argentina and invites the reader into Gambaro's collection of short stories.

Gambaro's Nosferatu, however, is an inversion of the traditional image of the deadly, powerful vampire. This Nosferatu has lost the power to kill and is weak and anemic. He is "deadly," not as an assassin, but in the sense that he himself embodies the dead, the dead who cannot rest. This is a Nosferatu in decomposition, a vampire in crisis, powerless and depressed:

> Pensó que se habían empequeñecido sus gestos, antes lo movía la pasión y ahora, cuando salía, consumaba un simple despojo, robaba como el más mísero de los ladrones y con menor aptitud. . . . Él, que había sido capaz de transformarse en criatura alada, estaba pegado a un cuerpo que le hablaba sólo de necesidad y no de gloria. (7–8)

> He felt that his gestures had diminished, he used to be driven by passion and now, when he went out, he'd only carry out one simple plunder, he stole like the most miserable of thieves and with less finesse. . . . He, who had once been able to transform himself into a winged creature, was confined to a body that spoke only of necessity and not of glory.

Thirsty for blood, Nosferatu scavenges at night and comes upon an older woman sifting through garbage bins for scraps to eat. She, like him, is desperately hungry. While approaching the elderly woman, Nosferatu feels faint and cannot follow through with his attack.

> Cuando llegó más cerca, comprendió que la vieja estaba inmovilizada por el hambre. Mientras que en él era sequedad, en ella el hambre rezumaba saliva, como en un animal esperando su alimento. Él pensó en atacarla, descubrió los colmillos y apresuró los últimos pasos, sabiendo no obstante que el simulacro no sustituiría la acción. Ya no podía atacar de esa manera, provocar el minuto de espanto y casi de amor que anticipaba en sus víctimas la entrega, el éxtasis pavoroso del deseo y de la muerte. (9)

> When he got closer, he understood that the old woman was paralyzed by hunger. While for him it was dryness, her hunger oozed saliva, like an animal waiting for its food. He thought about attacking her, he unveiled his fangs and quickened his step, knowing however that the simulacrum would not substitute for action. He could no longer attack that way, provoking a minute of fear and almost of love that he expected of his victims, the terrifying extasis of desire and death.

The woman does not perceive any danger and greets him. She holds out her hand and asks him whether he is okay. Nosferatu quietly gives her several bills and tries to go on his way. The elderly woman, however, is unsettled by Nosferatu's excessive generosity, and she follows him in an attempt to return some of the money, believing that he has made a mistake. Nosferatu refuses to accept any of the money, and she abandons it on the ground, hoping he will return for it; he never does.

He leaves her quickly and goes hungrily to a bar where he sits and shields his eyes from the light. He orders a glass of milk:

> Nosferatu se abalanzó hacia la leche y bebió. Tenía ganas de morder el vaso, pero ya no podía morder. No sabía por qué, quizá corrían otros tiempos, otras crueldades, y el gesto se había vuelto irrisorio. El líquido atemperó la sensación de vacío, la quemazón del hambre. Reclinándose contra el respaldo de la silla, suspiró y se dejó estar, como si él también pudiera adherirse a la frágil esperanza de los otros en la ventura posible, o más modestamente, compartiera la dicha de existir en la inadvertencia. (11)

> Nosferatu pounced on the milk and drank it. He wanted to bite the glass, but he could no longer bite. He didn't understand why, perhaps these were other times, other cruelties, and the gesture had become ridiculous. The liquid appeased the empty feeling, the burning hunger. Reclining against the back of the chair, he sighed and let go, as if he could also adhere as others to the fragile hope of potential happiness, or more modestly, as if he shared the fortune of careless existence.

He has lost his ability to bite, to sustain himself. For Nosferatu, "these were other times, other cruelties." His victims are faced with another phantom, crueler than he: they are already "living dead" in a society full of corruption that has left the poor digging for scraps. Aware of the elderly woman's hunger, Nosferatu is repulsed by his own attempt to kill her. Gambaro's Nosferatu is all but retired.

Just as he thinks to himself that he would like to lose himself in distractions, as others do, there enters a well-built officer who begins chasing him. As soon as they get outside (Nosferatu escapes through a window of the bar), he is being chased by a group of five fit young men. Nosferatu falls face down and his predators quickly grab him, turn him over, and pin him to the asphalt. He cannot escape the officers, who show their teeth and, in vampiric thirst, prey upon him.

These are "other times" in Argentina, and Gambaro's story is an allegory of a nation whose economy is steeped in debt accumulated, also, in "other times"; a nation whose wealth of natural resources and arable land should never leave a mouth unfed. Argentina, just as Nosferatu, is starved and at the mercy of others. Nosferatu also speaks to the power of authority figures who seek to kill the "undead" or the haunting memory of those who were disappeared in the Dirty War. The five officers are not emblematic of the ruin that Nosferatu embodies; they are young, strong, and uniformed. Their chasing down of Nosferatu is a metaphor of deliberately exorcising what remains of the past. These vampiric officers carry guns and track down Nosferatu beside a row of cars; they symbolize the postdictatorial means of the new replacing "the old without leaving a remainder" posited by Avelar. This imposition of forgetting upon a world marked by *memoria de sangre*, which cannot help but remember, sets the tone for the rest of the stories of *Lo mejor que se tiene*, in the aftermath and the ruins of postdictatorship Argentina.

The deliberate erasure of the past by more powerful figures is emphatically represented in "El trastocamiento" (Derangement). Traumatic memory, deceit, and the uncertainty of truth are primary themes in this story, in which a man visits Auschwitz for the second time. He had previously been a concentration camp prisoner, but now he is invited as a guest. His identity as prisoner or survivor of the death camp is disrupted or inverted, as the title *trastocamiento* denotes. *Trastocamiento* may be defined as a disruption, a disarranging of plans, and when referring to a person—*trastocarse*—may mean to go out of one's mind. Inversion is not only evident in the role of the survivor/guest, but also in the whole perception of Auschwitz itself. The concentration camp is referred to as "house" or "ranch," by the host. The host, as well, does not conform to the stereotypical features of the Aryan Gestapo soldier but appears to be an amiable man who guides the survivor/guest through the grounds.

In the opening paragraph, Gambaro implies the inescapability from trauma and its carnal prevalence:

> Sabía lo que iba a ver, lo que iba a encontrar. Todo padecimiento ya estaba impreso en él desde antes. Así que fue, no tranquilo sino doblemente perturbado, porque el dolor no se asentaría sobre la carne intacta, sin recuerdo, sino sobre el mismo dolor, antiguo, padecido. (81)

> He knew what he was going to see, what he would find there. All the suffering was already imbedded in him from before. So, he wasn't calm but twice as perturbed because the pain would not rest in his healed flesh, devoid of memory. Rather, it would settle upon the same old pain already suffered.

The mere thought of Auschwitz causes the initial suffering to resurface, and therefore the man is "twice as" perturbed by this visit. The past suffering and pain cannot be forgotten even if the physical body seems to have healed or the visual appearance of reality is inverted or absent. Furthermore, the libidinal memory, one that is physically initiated by the experience of the flesh in Auschwitz, cannot be prevented and the survivor/guest is doomed to reexperience the trauma of having been a prisoner in Auschwitz. Since the embodiment of remembering

Auschwitz is place-specific, the very place of the concentration camp, seemingly absent or not, is bound to the memory and act of suffering.

During this second visit, all the evidence of a concentration camp is absent and the guest/survivor is in a constant state of disbelief. "En vano se detuvo buscando la torre con los centinelas, los alambrados electrificados, los focos ciegos durante el día, implacables durante la noche" (81). [He stood in vain searching for the guards' lookout tower, the electrified fences, and the spotlights that are blind in the daytime but are impeccably efficient at night.] He searches restlessly for proof that he is indeed in Auschwitz. The guest/survivor cannot bear the lie he is witnessing: the beauty of the grounds, the playful children, the gracious manners of his host. Regardless of the cheerful singing and apparent tranquility he sees and hears, his intellect is victim to his relentless memory, and he is certain that the horrific face of suffering will reveal itself at any moment and the hoax will be inverted to represent reality:

> Pasaba gente por los campos, más allá del camino; parecían labradores y creyó escuchar un canto desparejo y feliz, pero no podía ser. Sabía que no podía ser porque ya había vivido esa experiencia en su carne o en sueños, y en cualquier momento lo que sabía se encajaría en el presente como una caja dentro de otra más grande. Escucharía insultos, gritos de dolor, y el interminable y amenazador aullido de los perros, acostumbrados al odio. (82)

> People walked along the fields, beyond the pathway; they looked like workers and he thought he heard a happy song, but it couldn't be. He knew it couldn't be because he had already lived the experience in his flesh and in his dreams, and at any moment everything he knew would encompass the present like a box within a larger one. He would hear insults, cries of agony, and the eternal and threatening howl of the dogs, who were accustomed to hatred.

The anticipation and lack of tangible evidence of the concentration camp cause the protagonist to experience a traumatic flashback, and he has an anxiety attack. He feels as though he is suffocating and clutches his arm thinking, it will soon be marked with indelible numbers inscribing his nameless identity. He resists breathing the air from outside which will inevitably be ashes from the crematorium and product of human flesh: "Quería salvarse, por lo menos esta segunda vez" (82). [He wanted to save himself, this second time at least.] The survivor/guest does all he can to protect himself from the torture that he cannot help but invoke in his memory. He is utterly deceived, however, upon taking a breath of air and smelling the freshly cut grass and flowers. His host begins to speak to him about music and art, but the guest/survivor is so overwhelmed by his traumatic flashback that he is sure everything will transform in an instant and he will be prisoner, pale and starving:

> No sólo cambiaría el decorado que lo rodeaba sino su propia calidad personal: de invitado pasaría a prisionero. Caerían sus ropas, sus cabellos, y se sumiría su carne en un ayuno de meses, y esperaba este acontecer pálido y convulso. (83)

> Not only had the decor that surrounded him changed but also his own personal identity: from guest he became prisoner. His clothes and hair would fall, and his flesh would sink from months without food, and pale and trembling he waited for this to happen.

This insistence that he is experiencing a hoax and will momentarily be taken back to the horrors of his tortured past speaks to Jean Améry's statement "Whoever was tortured, stays tortured" (1995 131). The survivor's past suffering does not allow space for trust or certainty, no matter how convincing the visual images of a changed reality may be. The disruption of what he perceives as "real" makes him feel as though he is losing his mind, and more than anything, he needs to see Auschwitz as he knows Auschwitz to be.

He follows his host through the "ranch" or "home," never referred to as "Auschwitz" or "concentration camp," and looks at the paintings, walls, and doors with utter disbelief:

> Pero él sabía lo que ocultaba Auschwitz, no discernía con qué fin el engaño de las apariencias, lo que sabía no podía borrarse. Detrás de esas puertas habría un depósito inmenso, construido con maderas húmedas y podridas, los camastros superpuestos, bajos, más justos que ataúdes, de donde sobresaldrían las grandes cabezas rapadas sostenidas por el esqueleto y el tul traslúcido de la piel, sólo vivos los ojos, redondos y móviles, como ojos de animales, la ansiedad o desesperación de vivir. (84)

> But he knew what Auschwitz was hiding. He didn't perceive to what end the trickery of appearances was intended. What he knew could not be erased. Behind those doors there was an immense storage constructed with moist and rotting wood—the beds were low and tighter than coffins; from them emerged large shaved heads attached to skeletons of translucent tulle skin. Only their round, mobile, and animal-like eyes were alive with the anxiety or desperation to live.

The real memories of Auschwitz pervade his body and sensory perception in such a way that he simply cannot bear the lie he seems to be wit-

nessing. His real memory of the emaciated skeletons of the concentration camp victims obstructs the survivor's perception so that he cannot
see beyond it and accept the inversion: "Cuando ya no pudo aguantar
más, no la incertidumbre, que nunca la había tenido, sino la desesperación de estar rodeado de dolor y no verlo. Se abalanzó hacia una
puerta y la abrió de golpe" (84). [When he could no longer stand it any-
more, not the uncertainty, which he had never had, but the desperation
of being surrounded by pain and not being able to see it. He rushed
toward a door and flung it open.] It is not the uncertainty that troubles
the guest, but rather his desperation for truth and confirmation that
urges him to open a door. Rather than finding what he knows as the
true horrors of Auschwitz, he finds laughing children playing, and his
host smiles on affectionately, as if nothing were going wrong at all. He
is trying to look at the suffering, trying to see the horror of the barely
living, but he is not permitted—the act of seeing is denied him just as
his identity as survivor is delegitimized.

Upon hearing music being played in another building on the
grounds, the visitor observes a woman and a man looking at each other
in utter happiness and the narrator acknowledges: "Vivían y ninguna
amenaza acechaba por encima de sus cabezas. Él sabía reconocer una
felicidad total, un estado sin miedos y sin estigmas, la paz de ventu-
rosas, intocables certidumbres para los días futuros" (86). [They were
living and not a single threat burdened them. He could sense complete
happiness, a state of being devoid of fear and stigmas, the peace of the
fortunate, untouchable assuredness about future days.] The young couple exudes total happiness; their complete lack of fear causes him to
question his perspective and almost to let down his defenses and accept
the inversion, but then the narrator recalls: "Estaba en Auschwitz y el
resto no tenía sentido" (86). [He was in Auschwitz and nothing else
mattered.]

His host leads him down another hallway and shows him into a small
white vacant room. Surprised not to see a whip, shiny boots, or syringes,
the guest looks at his host, perplexed. With total incomprehension, the
host asks, "¿Qué esperaba encontrar?" [What did you expect to see?]
The guest/survivor can no longer maintain his composure and runs
wildly through the corridors, fields, and paths, in an attempt to escape
the lie he has witnessed: "Gritó y saltó hacia la puerta. Abandonó la
pieza y corrió por los blancos corredores, atravesó el parque extra-
viando los senderos, dio vueltas enloquecido bajo un sol clemente y
mentiroso" (87). [He screamed and jumped toward the door. He raced
out of the room and ran down the white corridors; he ran across the

park ignoring the paths, and spun around crazed beneath the merciful and deceitful Sun.]

The narrator ends the story by implying that the only true escape would be in a dream—one that has no notion of reality. Gambaro further emphasizes the inability to escape from one's trauma, the fact that the survivor's reality is determined by his/her identity as survivor, and the need for the horrors of our history to be recognized by society. This denial of his identity in his "home" pushes the survivor to the margin. His marginalization is double, both external and internal. Having been a prisoner of Auschwitz, he was victim, marginalized by Aryan society, and marked for extermination. Now taken to his so-called home, which is obviously foreign and unfamiliar, one that he cannot connect with, he is also internally marginalized. Hence, he suffers an existential crisis from which there is "no exit" unless, of course, he is dreaming. The dream, however, exposes the tension between remembering and forgetting. The survivor's unconscious cannot help but remind him of his traumatic experience, which cannot be consciously worked through in an environment of denial.

"El trastocamiento" illustrates society's propensity to forget and hide gross realities and confirms the victim's inability to escape the truth that he has lived and carries forever branded upon his memory—the double-edged condition of having survived. The victim's inability to find any trace of the terror he had previously experienced at Auschwitz leaves him in a position of double marginality, of absolute solitude, that is unbearable—he becomes deranged, *se trastoca*. Such solitude, silence, and incomprehension by society can make a survivor's life impossible, and it is likely that such alienation led to the suicide of Holocaust survivors such as Jean Améry and Paul Celan. "El trastocamiento" recreates the tension between revealing and hiding, remembering and forgetting, that always characterizes traumatic history on both the individual and collective levels.

"El trastocamiento" does not suggest that Gambaro believes one may conflate the realities of the Dirty War and the Holocaust. In fact, the story was first published in 1968, a year after her play *El campo*, which also resuscitates images of the Nazi concentration camps. The "Dirty War" was not yet a part of the Argentine reality, but Onganía's dictatorship was, and it is evident that Gambaro's works of the 1960s—*Las paredes* (The Walls) (1963), *El desatino* (The Mistake) (1965), *Los siameses* (The Siamese) (1965), and *El campo* (The Camp) (1967)— were representing a society on the threshold of crisis, of decomposition. It is, however, very timely that such a striking narrative as "El trastocamiento" should have been republished in the aftermath of the Dirty War, at a time when President Carlos Menem had granted amnesty to convicted military officials and was pushing for Argentina to close the doors on the past.

Gambaro is responding precisely to this denial of discourse and memory of the past. This story of masking reality serves as a signifier for the encouragement to forget the horrors that took place in clandestine prisons during the Dirty War, and the guest/survivor's desperation serves as allegory to represent the traumatized Argentine population's need to admit and openly remember their historical reality: those who survived the clandestine prisons of the Dirty War, those whose loved ones were disappeared, those who have returned from exile, those who continue in exile, and the generations to come.

Gambaro's play *La casa sin sosiego* (The Haunted House) (1991) may be interpreted as a sequel to "El trastocamiento." Teresa is missing and Juan frantically searches for her. No one openly tells Juan where she is or what has happened to her. At a local bar he asks a few men whether they remember having seen her. Their response is "Nada recordamos / Porque no miramos" (38). [We don't remember anything / Because we don't look.] Meanwhile, Teresa repeats to herself, while in the *loquero, mad-house:* "Memoria, memoria, casa de pena / Nadie quiere habitarla / y allí me dejan / Memoria, memoria, casa de pena / ¿Quién me trajo a este lugar de tinieblas?" (39). [Memory, memory, house of pain / No one wants to live in it / and they leave me there / Memory, memory, house of pain / Who brought me to this dark place?] Memory is a solitary space of suffering in Gambaro's work published in the postdictatorship era. Just as the guest/survivor of "El trastocamiento" is driven to madness in a world that denies his experience, Teresa is hidden away in an asylum.

The guest/survivor in "El trastocamiento" is looking for physical evidence of Auschwitz—emaciated bodies lumped together, the stacks of the crematorium, ashes—and he is denied any proof. The physical world of decomposing bodies that was Auschwitz has become invisible, except to the survivor, who cannot escape the throes of his memory, or his *casa de pena*. Because of the physicality of the horrors also suffered in the Dirty War—torture, mutilated bodies, mass graves, bodies dropped from planes into the Río de la Plata—we may also read "El trastocamiento" as a representation of the invisibility with regard to Argentina's Dirty War, of the "disappeared" who cannot be claimed because of the silencing by repressive forces and the absence of bodies. Furthermore, if we consider that Madres and Abuelas demanding their

disappeared children reappear alive—they carried banners stating
"aparición con vida"—were called *locas* by the military junta, the term
trastocarse may well apply to what these women felt in the face of a society that would simply not listen to them.

Another Gambaro play, also from 1991, *Atando cabos* (Tying Loose
Ends), is dedicated to the victims of La noche de los lápices (The Night
of Pencils) and centers on the tension between remembering and forgetting.[8] The play is a dialogue between a mother, Elisa, whose fifteen-
year-old daughter was thrown from a helicopter into the Río de la Plata,
and Martín, whom the mother meets while on a boat. When Elisa
accuses Martín of seeming militarylike and implies that he may have
been involved in the junta, Martín refuses to take responsibility for the
cruel acts of the dictatorship and refuses to listen to Elisa's story about
her daughter. He says: "Nunca vi. Quien saltó al mar, al río, fue porque
se lo buscó. Si un pajarito se para bajo la pata de un elefante, será aplastado. Me refiero naturalmente a su hija" (18). [I never saw. Those who
jumped into the sea, the river, asked for it. If a bird stands in front of
an elephant's hoof, it'll be smashed. Obviously, I'm referring to your
daughter.] Evidently, Gambaro is criticizing the populace's compliance
with the terror reaped by the regime, and Martín's response makes a
statement about the common phrases circulating throughout Argentina
during the era: "Por algo será" (it happened for some reason) and "Algo
habrá hecho" (s/he must have done something). Such statements
denied any collective responsibility for the disappearance of individuals and further contributed to the regime's ability to fragment the
Argentine society into subversives and accomplices/supporters of the
dictatorship, even if citizens did not consciously realize that their passivity contributed to the construction and dissemination of fear.

When they are saved from their lifeboat, Martín asks whether he'll
ever see Elisa again and he blames their tense conversation on his
nerves, insisting that he is innocent. Elisa responds:

> Usted lo dijo, inocente como son los que tienen la fuerza. Algo haré para
> que no deje de verme. En tierra, en el naufragio. Algo haré para no deje de
> verme. . . . Hablaré tanto que lo inundaré con mi memoria, y no podrá res-
> pirar, y se ahogará en tierra, ¡en el naufragio! . . . No conseguir borrar mi
> memoria, su naufragio. En esta tierra que transito usted no puede vivir. En
> estas aguas, usted no sabe nadar. (26)

> You said it yourself, innocent as those in power. I'll do something so that
> you never cease to see me. On land, shipwrecked. I'll do something so you
> never cease to see me. . . . I'll speak so much that I'll drown you with the

memory of me, and you won't be able to breathe, and you'll drown on earth, shipwrecked! . . . Your shipwreck, unable to erase the memory of me. On this land that I travel you cannot live. In these waters, you do not know how to swim.

Elisa's stern message to Martín affirms that the day will arrive when he must face the truth about the death flights and be held accountable for the atrocious crimes of the Dirty War, which have been pardoned. *Memoria de sangre* will not vanish. Mothers such as Elisa will relentlessly keep memory alive and fight for recognition and justice. Those who are forgetful and in denial will drown. It is ironic that Martín should use the elephant as a symbol of the authoritative junta, for on the contrary, the elephant symbolizes memory and it will eventually be the deniers of the past, the likes of Martín, who will be flattened, *aplastado*, by the persistence of memory.

The survivor/guest's internal exile, that of not being acknowledged at "home," may be considered in the light of an excerpt from Primo Levi's *Survival in Auschwitz*, in which he gives testimony to his nightmare of trying to narrate his survival, the "unlistened-to" story:

This is my sister here, with some unidentifiable friend and many other people. They are all listening to me and it is this very story that I am telling: the whistle of three notes, the hard bed. My neighbor whom I would like to move, but whom I am afraid to wake as he is stronger than me. I also speak diffusely of our hunger and of the lice-control, and of the Kapo who hit me on the nose and then sent me to wash myself as I was bleeding. It is an intense pleasure, physical, inexpressible, to be at home, among friendly people and to have so many things to recount: but I cannot help but notice that my listeners do not follow me. In fact, they are completely indifferent: they speak confusedly of other things among themselves, as if I were not there. My sister looks at me, gets up and goes away without a word. (60)

Such indifference is ultimate torture for the survivor who must externalize his experience in order to exist among others in the *aftermath*. Levi goes on to tell that this is a recurring dream he cannot escape: "My dream stands in front of me, still warm, and although awake, I am still full of its anguish: and then I remember that it is not a haphazard dream, but that I have dreamed it not once but many times since I arrived here, with hardly any variations of environment or details. . . . Why does it happen? Why is the pain of every day translated so constantly into our dreams, in the ever-repeated scene of the unlistened-to story?" (60) The indifference and unwillingness to listen to Levi's story create his "pain of every day" since he has survived Auschwitz. His unconscious is burdened both by the experiences of the *lager* and by the indifference he encounters upon having survived. The "pain of every day"—of not being listened to—denies him of his past, of claiming his status of victim and survivor, and of raising others' consciousness. This pain is "a desolating grief [that] is now born in me. . . . It is pain in its pure state . . . a pain like that which makes children cry" (Levi 60). The pain that "makes children cry" is the anguish of not being heard, of feeling abandoned and deserted. In Chaim Guri's film *The Eighty-first Blow*, it is precisely the denial of a survivor's narrative by his audience that casts the mortal eighty-first blow, beyond which he cannot survive. There is nothing worse, for Levi, for the survivor in Guri's film, and for the guest/survivor in "El trastocamiento" than being denied narrative space—than being denied their identity as victims/survivors—than being "unlistened-to" by an *addressable other* who can affirm the survival story and further carve a place in society for the survivor to feel a sense of belonging.

The protagonist of Gambaro's "Buscando la compañía del árbol" also carries an "unlistened-to" story. Because society rejects her suffering, she is unable to develop a language with which to externalize her pain. The essential themes of "Buscando la compañía del árbol" are longing for community, yearning for a narrative and an *addressable other*, and the breakdown of language. This *buscando*, or seeking, speaks to the desperate search for a language with which to communicate the "unspeakable"—that which is so painful that it leaves us at a loss for words—and for the search of an empathic listener.

As Primo Levi writes in *If Not Now, When?*, "our language lacks words to express this offense, the demolition of a man" (9). The terror of the concentration camps of the Dirty War, though of course different from that of the camps of Nazi extermination, also entailed a systematic method of applying torture and exterminating prisoners. Marguerite Feitlowitz's *Lexicon of Terror: Argentina and the Legacies of Torture*, through testimony gathered during interviews of camp survivors, denounces the breakdown of language within the Argentine clandestine prison system, the concentration camps, and within Argentine society as a whole. In an interview Feitlowitz conducted with Mario Villani, who was kept in clandestine prisons from 1977 to 1981, he speaks of an outing he and several pregnant women prisoners of the Olympus prison were allowed to Chacabuco Park and a nearby café. While at the café, Mario feared that they might be overheard by other civilians sitting around them, but then he realized: "No one could have understood what we were talking about—we were speaking in code, as it were. Not deliberately, it was just how we spoke then. And it hit me: Here I am, sitting at a café—out in the world, but not a part of it. Not a member" (83). By citing Villani, Feitlowitz stresses the importance of language for creating bridges between the individual and the collective, for fostering a sense of belonging and community.

The isolation created by the breakdown of language, the wounding of a once common lexicon, is a form of continuous repression of, which society must work to heal. Feitlowitz states:

> The repression lives on in such aberrations of the language, in the scars it left on the language. When a people's very words have been wounded, the society cannot fully recover until the language has been healed. Words mark the paths of our experience, separate what we can name from ineffable terror and chaos. At once public and intimate, language is a boundary between our vulnerable inner selves and the outside world. When, like skin, the language is bruised, punctured, or mutilated, that boundary breaks down. We have then no defense, no way to protect ourselves. What we knew, we no longer know; names born of the truth of shared experience ring false. *On a mal dans sa peau*—we are uneasy in our own skin. (62)

It is a common language, one that connects with the "outside world" that Villani must nurture in order to belong to community once again. Hiding his experience, however, will not lead to "healing" but to denial. Feitlowitz's argument is that the collective society must take responsibility for the healing of language because it is the whole that is wounded and must recover so that the "vulnerable inner selves" of the individual may be understood by the collective language of the "outside world."

Healing a wounded language places great responsibility not only on the speaker, but on the listener to that which is ineffable. We must consider that society's refusal to listen to traumatic history contributes to the inability to engender a language with which to communicate such an offense. Susan Brison asserts: "We need not only the words with which to tell our stories, but also an audience able and willing to hear us and to understand our words as we intend them. This aspect of remaking a self in the aftermath of trauma highlights the dependency of the self on others and helps to explain why it is so difficult for survivors to recover when others are unwilling to listen to what they endured (51). Brison aptly states that the audience, the listener, must be able and willing to suspend the boundary of language, and to hear our words as we intend them even if they are not the most appropriate and conventional choices. The important role that others or *empathic listeners* have in aiding one "remake" him/herself in the aftermath of trauma is precisely what "Buscando la compañía del árbol" begs the reader to consider. Why does the young woman in the story seek solace from a tree and not from another person?

In this story, a newborn is denied the ability to cry. She does, however, unleash an alarming wail that surfaces from a profound inner sadness that she carries within. The young girl is silent because her language is never understood by those around her. She does, however, attempt to communicate, and therefore her cries and her intolerable wail are her voice.

Although alive, she is seemingly possessed by death and may thus be read as a vessel of those who have died and suffered repression. She writhes with the repressed voices of those who have gone before her, perhaps even of those vampiric spirits of "unfinished mourning." Their silence will find their voice or their scream through her. Only an infant, she instills terror in her own mother:

> Se dormía casi, cuando oyó un sonido que la despertó y erizó sus cabellos. La niña gemía, los ojos cerrados. La vela oscilaba y el cuarto se llenaba de sombras. Apoyó al niño recién nacido en la cuna y se inclinó sobre ella, con el rostro ceniciento. Ningún niño podía gemir de esa manera salvo que la muerte le retorciera las entrañas. Y recordó que al nacer no había entrado al mundo con lágrimas sino con un lamento semejante, aullido ronco que les había hecho pensar que moriría. (54)

> She was almost asleep when she heard a sound that woke her and set her hairs on end. The little girl groaned with her eyes closed. The candle wavered and the room filled with shadows. She laid the newborn in his crib and leaned over her daughter with her ashen face. No child could moan that way unless death writhed within her. And she remembered that at birth her daughter hadn't entered the world with tears but rather with a similar lament, a hoarse moan that had made them think she was dying.

A seemingly uncanny bond with death, filling the room with shadows, has marked this young girl. From the onset of her life, she suffers in a way that frightens her own mother, thus denying the child the affection given to her other siblings: "Empezó a considerarla con sospecha y guardó celosamente el secreto que había descubierto aquella noche. No podía abrazarla como a sus otros hijos, ni la niña se arrojaba a sus brazos como ellos, que sin cesar reclamaban esa cuota de amor" (54). [She began to be suspicious of her and she jealously kept the secret she had discovered that night. She could not embrace her as she did her other children, nor did the girl throw herself into her arms as did the others, who constantly demanded that quota of love.] Only a toddler, she is already pushed to the margins of her own family. She is different from the other children and her own mother is suspicious of her.

Not only does this girl lack the words with which to express the trauma that haunts her, but she has no audience to whom she may express herself. The secret her mother conceals is the "unspeakable" that the mother also knows and that terrifies her; it is that element which makes the young girl the abject and rejected by those closest to her.

The first time she injures herself, when she is still an infant, her mother protects the other children from their sister in anticipation of the moribund wail:

> La madre los apartó hacia el rincón más alejado de la cocina, sumido casi en la oscuridad. Por primera vez desde aquella ocasión en la cuna de tablas, brotó de sus labios esa queja incómoda que recordaba cosas de una materia corrompida . . ., como la visión de un cadáver sacado de su tumba. (55)

> The mother pushed them toward the farthest corner of the kitchen, almost submerged in darkness. For the first time since the wooden crib, her lips unleashed that uncomfortable cry recalling rotten things . . ., like the vision of a cadaver disinterred from its grave.

Unintentionally, for she is unable to cry simply as other children do, this girl casts death all around with her indescribable grief. Childhood, seemingly remote from death, is cursed in the one who screams of rotten things. Just as a cadaver pulled from its grave, this girl terrifies her family as might a ghost or a vampire, unable to rest because of aberrant mourning. When her siblings begin to cry out of fear, her father slaps her and orders her to stop her wailing: "Y ella hubiera querido decirle, en su media lengua, que ése era su llanto, que de algún modo aceptara su llanto y la consolara" (55–56). [And she would have liked to have told him, in her half language, that that was her cry, and that he should somehow accept her cry and console her.] Unable to express her need for her father's acceptance and understanding verbally, she continues her lament until he hits her much harder than before and silences her. Such a violent response to the girl's desire and attempt to communicate with her father stunts the potential for her to develop her "half language" and engender any understanding among her own family. Again, the violent response by her father speaks to the absence of empathy, or any space of externalization of this "materia corrompida" that the girl must contend with alone.

She is the figure of the abject, and her family cannot approach her. As the rejection escalates and often results in brutality, the girl protects herself by hiding her misery and mourning privately, holding in her cry:

> Entonces se acostumbró a engañar; disimulando su dolor, aprendió a guardarlo dentro de una caja cerrada que era ella misma; como a un animal invisible, le suplicaba paciencia hasta que pudiera soltarlo en soledad. Sonreía si se golpeaba mientras su madre y sus hermanos la observaban recelosos, casi con miedo, y todos pensaban: ahora comenzará a gemir; se paralizaban, la respiración suspendida, prontos a huir en tropel para no escuchar esa queja que les hablaba de lo innombrable. (56)

> She then began to fake it; dissimulating her pain, she learned to store it inside a sealed box, which she had become; as if her pain were an invisible animal, she begged it to be patient until she could release it in solitude. She smiled if she injured herself while her mother and siblings observed her jealously, almost in fear, and they all thought: "Now she'll begin to moan." They froze, holding their breath, on the verge of running away in a herd so as not to hear that which spoke of the unspeakable.

The *innombrable* or "unspeakable" that instills such fear, and that no one can bear to witness, is the only voice this young girl has. To her family and the villagers, she is a vessel of evil and of a truth that no one dares to acknowledge. The fragmentation of the familial and social sphere as a result of the uncanny serves as allegory for the fragmentation of Argentine society in the face of fear instilled by the authoritarian regime. As Carina Perelli asserts in her essay "Memoria de sangre": "To force the population to reach this condition was the ultimate goal of the state-controlled and managed terror apparatus in Argentina. It not only reduced citizens to obedience but also utterly destroyed the possibility of emergence of a horizontal voice by abolishing the essence of the dialogical principle. By shattering the bridges of connectedness and empathy, this culture of fear reduced society to a set of separate individuals living their atomized lives under the supervision of all-powerful authorities" (45). Her inability to articulate her pain with a common cry, or with language, ensures its unsharability and leads to misunderstanding.[9]

This tortured woman needs a listener, for her pain cannot possibly diminish without a compassionate and sensitive other. As asserted by LaCapra and Laub, in order to recover from trauma, one must reexternalize the traumatic event by constructing a narrative and sharing it with an empathic listener. This narrative, or testimony, as Laub suggests, is not a monologue: "[Testimonies] cannot take place in solitude. The witnesses are talking to *somebody:* to somebody they have been waiting for for a long time" (1992 70–71). With no one to talk to, this victim remains "entrapped" in trauma repetition and cannot move on from her suffering. By protecting themselves from "lo innombrable," her family and neighbors (potential witnesses of the girl's testimony) increase the girl's suffering and sense of isolation.

This neglect prevents her from potentially discovering a language with which to describe her grief, and she begins deserting her village when overwhelmed with sadness and anticipating a cry. "Buscaba sin saber qué, y aunque gemía en medio del campo, erguida y sola, le parecía que su queja era más desesperada en ese paisaje sin apoyo" (57). [She searched not knowing what for, and even though she writhed in the middle of the field, upright and alone, her cry seemed more desperate in that unsupportive landscape.] One day, farther away from her home than she had gone before, she discovers an enormous tree among the rocks and seeks solace in it:

> Con una sorpresa llena de gratitud descubrió un árbol de tronco grueso y hojas verdes que se alzaba solitario entre las piedras. Corrió hacia él, apoyó la mejilla en el tronco. Y a partir de ese día cada vez que una aflicción la asaltaba, buscaba el árbol y bajo lo que creía era su amparo, lanzaba su lamento. (57)

> With surprise full of gratitude she discovered a solitary tree with a wide trunk and green leaves among the rocks. She ran toward it and leaned her cheek against its trunk. From that day forward she sought the tree any time she was overcome by grief and, beneath what she believed to be her protector, she unleashed her lament.

She is relieved to find a recipient for her tremendous sadness and to feel somewhat protected. But even the tree cannot tolerate the anguish she suffers and loses its verdure little by little, until even its wide trunk breaks in half and crashes to the ground. The loss of her only companion is unbearable; she cries so loud and long that even the sky begins to darken.

Gambaro's story recalls the Chilean author María Luisa Bombal's "El árbol," in which a rubber tree, a *gomero,* enchants Brígida, whose only true space of happiness is in the dressing room where she feels sheltered by the tree that is reflected in the mirrors lining the room. Brígida, similar to the girl in "Buscando," was treated with neglect by her father, who called her retarded and preferred not to be bothered by her. Now married, but not for love, she feels utterly alone. She finds solace in the *gomero*, in which "una podía pasarse las horas muertas, vacía de todo pensamiento, atontada de bienestar" (162) [one could waste hours, thoughtlessly, happily numb], until the day it is cut down and Brígida's dressing room is suddenly invaded by all the elements from which the *gomero* had shielded her. The death of the tree forces her to move on and liberate herself. Brígida leaves her husband and we meet her much later while she listens to Mozart and recalls the *gomero*.

Seemingly alone with her pain and her unbearable cry, the young woman of "Buscando" suddenly notices a young boy observing her. He is barefoot and ragged, and his skin is marked with scars. She runs from him, reaches what remains of the tree that had fallen, and releases a tremendous howl. As the remaining stub of the tree crumbles to the ground and the sky darkens, the rough yet tender hand of the young boy touches her cheek and he asks her why she is crying. Suddenly, her wail becomes a tolerable river of tears and the young woman's misery is lighter—an *other* to whom she may give testimony now exists. The young boy's gesture fills an intolerable void in this woman's life—that of living in utter solitude and lack of compassion and comprehension by all others. This very simple yet profound gesture of approaching the pained other has saved her from madness and perhaps even suicide. The connection with another being "remakes" her as part of a community, albeit a very small one, but a community nonetheless. This act of compassion speaks to Elaine Scarry's work regarding the pain of torture: "As torture consists of acts that magnify the way in which pain destroys a person's world, self, and voice, so these other acts that restore the voice become not only a denunciation of the pain but almost a diminution of the pain, a partial reversal of the process of torture itself . . . sympathy lessens the power of sickness and pain" (50).

How is it that this girl is born with such immense grief? As far as the story tells us, she bore her trauma since birth. She does not bear physical scars similar to those of the boy who reaches out to her in the wilderness. So, the reader is left to speculate that this trauma is inherited by the young girl—she embodies the psychological trauma of unfinished mourning. I venture to suggest that her inability to cry, to narrate her trauma (her silence), and her intolerable moan recalling fetid representations of death embody past destruction and silencing of the Dirty War. She is the tension that is both the inability and the need to forget, the inability and the need to remember. It is this in-betweenness and ambiguity that do not respect borders and disturb identity that cause abjection.[10] Her physical beauty is betrayed by the putrefaction that is her wail. She longs to find a voice but is silenced by her family and neighbors, who refuse to listen, who will not allow her to find a language with which to develop her narrative, who deny the past. She is the representative of a society that has survived "unspeakable" destruction and may be read as the manifestation of the "unmentionable years" described by Nadine Fresco in her work about children of Holocaust survivors: "the gaping, vertiginous black hole of the unmentionable years. . . . The silence formed like a heavy pall that weighed down on everyone. Parents explained nothing, children asked nothing. The forbidden memory of death manifested itself only in the form of incomprehensible attacks of pain" (418). Supported by this reading, we must hear a polyphony of voices in the girl's cry. Nicolás Abraham's theory of the transgenerational phantom suggests precisely this existence of a collective psychology of several generations within the individual.[11] The phantom is passed from one generation to the next unconsciously and "works like a ventriloquist, like a stranger within the subject's own mental topography" (173). Gambaro's protagonist is the embodiment of the "transgenerational phantom" who unknowingly carries the past that is not spoken of, that which is taboo. She is signifier of that which is forbidden, for she is forbidden to speak, and no one but the scarred boy in the forest, who physically embodies suffering, willingly listens to the representation of trauma that the girl cannot help but exhale. And it is entrapped within this "desolate grief" that the child of survivors, the society that is "uneasy in its own skin," will remain until testimony is given and the silence is ruptured.

Within the panorama of works that are Gambaro's so-called theater of crisis, we may also infer that the girl of "Buscando la compañía del árbol" is carrying on the pained cries of Dolores of *La malasangre* (Bad Blood) (1981) and Oscar of *Del sol naciente* (Of the Rising Sun) (1984). Both *La malasangre* and *Del sol naciente* end with screams of anguish. In contrast to some of Gambaro's earlier plays, in which the victim is silenced, Dolores of *La malasangre* is rebellious against her authoritarian father and refuses to be silenced. When her father insists that she be quiet, she retorts: "El silencio grita! Yo me callo, pero el silencio grita!" [Silence screams! I'll be quiet, but silence screams!] As the play comes to an end, Dolores's shouting continues in a prolonged wail. The girl who is "Buscando la compañía del árbol" is silenced but cannot contain the "hauntingly possessive ghosts" that are the trauma that precedes her birth.

Therefore, her silence screams, as Dolores insists to her father, and manifests itself in the "incomprehensible attacks of pain" described by Fresco.

After drowning Oscar in the play *Del sol naciente*, the totalitarian Obán hears a cry from somewhere and asks: "Y ahora, de muertos, quieren tener voz. Oí el gemido. ¿Qué me hará este gemido? Esta tierra de pelagatos está llena de gemidos" (150–51). [Now that they're dead they wish to speak. I heard the moaning. What will that moan do to me? This land full of scarecrows is full of muffled cries]. Though dead, evidently Oscar will haunt Obán and the land that has been sown with injustice. The girl of "Buscando," although alive, is seemingly possessed by death; she is a vessel of those who have died and suffered repression. Their disappearance and improper burial will find their voice or their scream through her "half language," which can only heal once society as a whole takes responsibility for healing its wound.

The presence of the boy who is physically scarred gives the woman a space to narrate her suffering. His scars mark his otherness, distinguishing him from those who refuse to acknowledge the woman's pain. As Brooks states: "One cannot read, as one cannot cure, from the outside. It is only through assuming the burden and the risks of the transferential situation that one reaches the understanding of otherness" (70). Just as the reader wonders what it is that ails the young woman and wishes to establish a dialogic relationship with her, the boy becomes listener, reader, and analyst, eliciting a narrative and therefore lifting a burden from the woman who *needs* to share her story. It is significant that the boy wears physical scars that differentiate his pain from that of the womans. The boy's scars announce his otherness and openness to empathize with the woman's pain, but because of their difference, do not threaten to claim her suffering as his own, therefore complying with LaCapra's definition of the "secondary witness."

The protagonist of "El encuentro" (The Encounter) suffers from a known loss, that of her brother, and also yearns for an empathic other. Her sense of lack is such that she appropriates her loss and sees her brother embodied by other young boys. This story speaks to the experience of loss and the fantastic effects of nostalgia and melancholy that erase the boundaries of time and place. Ana experiences what Freud calls "a turning away from reality"[12] as she refuses to abandon libidinal attachments to her brother; she clings to her memory of him through the medium of young boys who resemble him. Trapped in a stage of melancholia, Ana cannot distinguish between the past and the present. She "acts out" by regenerating the past as if it were fully present.[13]

Ana's mourning of her brother's death is marked by her nostalgic childhood memory of playing together, a memory that resurfaces when she sees young boys who activate her libidinal attachment to him. While awaiting her flight in an airport, Ana sees a young boy who reminds her of her dead, or perhaps disappeared, brother. There is no mention of the way he died, but we do know that he was older than she. Ana's eyes are fixed on the boy in the airport, and a process of doubling and regeneration takes place within the scopic field that is her gaze. Utilizing Lacan's definition of the gaze, in which, "in our relation to things, in so far as this relation is constituted by the way of vision, and ordered in the figures of representation, something slips, passes, is transmitted, from stage to stage" (73), I suggest that Ana also transmits elements of her trauma to the young boy who is her object of encounter. A Lacanian reading of this encounter would also propose that, for the boy, this meeting intiates what Lacan calls *beánce*, a rupture—the boy who had been living in the *jovial* substage now passes into a fragmentary stage where the secure world he had once imagined is not such. Although "El encuentro" does lend itself to such analysis, Gambaro does not allow the reader the narrative satisfaction of seeing the repercussions of this meeting for the boy.

She recalls her brother's photo and notices the physical similarities between him and the young boy in the airport:

> El niño parecía a su hermano, en aquella fotografía color sepia, cuando había tomado la primera comunión. Se parecía de un modo casi mortificante, tenía la misma expresión, tímida y triste, los ojos oscuros y las orejas separadas del cráneo. Ana sabía que cuando el niño creciera las orejas no resultarían tan grandes ni separadas. Lo miró largamente, como si su hermano estuviera allí, niño de nuevo. Su hermano estaba sentado, la expresión tímida y triste, en una incómoda silla del aeropuerto. (179)

> The boy looked like her brother, in that sepia colored photo from his first communion. The resemblance was almost mortifying; he had the same expression, shy and sad, the dark eyes and the ears that stuck out. Ana knew that when the boy got older his ears wouldn't seem as big. She looked at him a long while, as if her brother were there, a boy again. Her brother was sitting, with shy and sad expression, in an uncomfortable airport seat.

The photo, similar to Bortnik's "Cuatro fotos," has become a trace of life and a marker of death—as is the encounter with a child resembling her brother—a source of hope, a resurrection of her memory of her brother, and a painful reminder of his death. Marianne Hirsch's statement resounds in this story: "It is precisely the indexical nature of the photo, its status as relic, or trace, or fetish—its 'direct' connection with the material presence of the photographed person—that at once intensifies its status as harbinger of death and, at the same time and concomitantly, its capacity to signify life" (20). Projection takes place in the gaze Ana casts upon this young boy. His sad, shy expression becomes that of her brother since she projects her brother's sadness onto the young boy, as if he were a screen. Although, as mentioned, the reader cannot glimpse the boy's future, this slippage would appear to burden the boy with posthumous history or perhaps with Abraham's notion of the "transgenerational phantom" that is unconsciously passed on, a phantom that may only resurface unrecognized by the young boy.

While he is the target of her gaze, the young boy also unknowingly helps Ana resurrect her brother. He becomes her brother's double, and she revisits her childhood memories: "Ese niño que se parecía a su hermano despertaba en ella una fuerte nostalgia" (179). [That boy that resembled her brother made her feel deeply nostalgic.] Her nostalgia is such that she also questions whether the boy's sister could also be her own double:

> La niña trató de llevar una vez más la falda por debajo de las rodillas, luego renunció, el rostro enfurruñado. Sus cabellos negros caían en rulos sobre los hombros, semejantes a los de Ana en otra época, pero a Ana no le habían sacado fotos como a su hermano en la primera comunión, y no podía saber si también la niña se le parecía a la edad remota de sus cinco años. (181)

> The little girl tried to pull her skirt below her knees once again, then gave up, her face sullen. Her black hair fell in curls over her shoulders, similar to Ana's at one time, but they hadn't taken a picture of Ana as they had of her brother during his first communion, and so she couldn't tell if the girl also resembled her at the remote age of five years old.

Although Ana is uncertain whether the girl is indeed her young self, she does not discard the possibility. Her refusal to let go of her attachment to her brother allows her to reenter her memory of the "nonliving world" and makes way for the fantastic trope of intersecting lives in "El encuentro."[14] The airport becomes a space where the blurring of time and place occurs. The *encuentro*, the encounter, is a reencounter with her childhood, but it is also a missed encounter with a world that eludes her, one that is no longer living.

Ana tries to combat her obsession with the young boy, but her attempt at resistance fails. His uncanny resemblance to the photo draws her to him:

No quería mirar al niño, pero otra vez volvió a clavar los ojos en él y la invadió el mismo sentimiento, mezcla de dolor y de asombro. Le recordaba tanto a su hermano en aquella fotografía de comunión, sentado sobre una banqueta, las manos enguantadas sosteniendo el breviario, la expresión tímida y triste, iluminada por un rayo de luz. Y el parecido era tan grande que hubiera querido abrazar a ese niño, como cada día había deseado hacerlo con su hermano, que había muerto no hacía mucho y a quien no podría abrazar nunca más. La inmaterialidad de la muerte, que nos arrebata el cuerpo, la acongojó. (182)

She did not want to look at the boy, but her eyes fixed upon him again and she was overcome with that same feeling, a combination of pain and wonder. He reminded her so much of her brother in that communion photograph, sitting on a bench, his gloved hands holding the breviary, his shy and sad expression, illuminated by a ray of light. And the similarity was so strong that she wanted to embrace that boy, as every day she wished to embrace her brother, who died not long ago and who she could never again embrace. The immateriality of death, that snatches the body from us, saddened her.

This passage is riddled with signifiers that speak beyond the reality that is the airport. The mention that her brother had died "not long ago," a temporal marker also used in Gambaro's play *Antígona furiosa* (Furious Antigone), denouncing the disappeared of the Dirty War, could situate her brother temporally as a victim of the dictatorship era. Further, Gambaro's use of *nunca más* (never again) in the very same sentence explicitly recalls the title *Nunca más* of the testimonies of the Dirty War victims collected by the CONADEP. The narrator speaks of the "immateriality of death," hinting at the absence of a body to mourn, perhaps the absence of a "disappeared" person. Upon saying that this immateriality of death snatches the body from *us*, the narrator coerces the reader into the experience of loss. Therefore, the loss may be perceived as a collective experience. The absence of a name with which to individualize Ana's brother and his ready association with others further support my argument that his death is one of a collective nature, situating him among the 30,000 disappeared who are too many to name.

"El encuentro," in its denunciation of a wrongful death, recalls Gambaro's play *Antígona furiosa* and its representations of the Dirty War.

Diana Taylor argues that Gambaro chooses to use Antigone to represent this history because the "Antigone plot specifically raises questions about political leadership and misrule, about the conflict between the so-called private and public spaces, about public fear and complicity, about a population's duty to act as a responsible witness to injustice, and about social practices and duties predicated on sexual difference that were as urgent during the Dirty War as they were in 441 BC. (1997 209). In the ancient play, "characters speak to us from the far side of death" (209). Antigone is enraged about the death of her brother, Polinices; Creon's policies; and the impossibility of giving her brother a proper burial. Antigone of the 1986 play cannot come to terms with the brutality and pure cruelty she is faced with, and she hangs herself. In the short story, however, An[tígon]a is in the process of mourning, in which occasionally the past and present overlap. The impossibility of accepting death—the difficulty of mourning and the trauma of loss— lead Ana to draw links between young boys and her dead brother and question the possibility of intersecting lives.

Other details of the story further situate this unidentified collective loss in the margin. Ana was once reproached by a mother who did not tolerate Ana's interest in the woman's young child:

> Se había interpuesto entre Ana y el niño, enfrentándola con ostensible hostilidad y un sentimiento de aversión en los fulminantes ojos, límpidos y azules. En aquel entonces, ella había lamentado su inglés insuficiente para explicar que su intención era benévola, aunque si hubiera sido eficaz y fluido, tampoco lo habría hecho. Rápidamente supo que esa madre blanca, de piel casi translúcida, bien vestida, no comprendería nunca el sentido de ninguna mirada. (183)

> She intervened between Ana and the boy, confronting her with ostensible hostility and aversion in her fulminating eyes, clear and blue. At the time she was sorry her English was too poor to explain that she had good intentions, even though she wouldn't have done it even if it was fluent and precise. She quickly realized that that white mother, of almost translucent skin, and well dressed, would never understand the meaning of any gaze.

This upper-class English-speaking mother could not comprehend Ana's nostalgic gaze that spoke of loss, which Ana could not articulate. Language, class, and history are barriers that distance Ana from this woman. The aversion that the mother expresses to Ana with her strikingly cold blue eyes alienates Ana. The narrator comments that even if

Ana could speak English fluently, she would not have spoken to the mother. Language is not enough to make the *other* understand her loss. The mother embodies an authoritative power who silences the subaltern. The child, however, the object of Ana's gaze, will bear a past that is yet unknown to him, a posthumous history that Ana has transmitted to him unconsciously.

This time, however, the mother of the young children in the airport is much more understanding and trusting of Ana:

> Ésta era gorda, inelegante, ordinaria en su pobreza ancestral, pero no se abroquelaba en el amor como la otra para alimentar suspicacias y recelos, ésta no temía, no sólo sus miradas, tampoco el roce de una mano sobre su criatura. Y quizás algo intuía también de pérdidas ajenas, del vano deseo de resurrección. (183)

> This one was fat, inelegant, common in her ancestral poverty, but she didn't shield herself from love in order to feed suspicions and jealousies like the other one; this one did not fear, not only looks, but neither a hand touching her child. And maybe she also intuited others' losses, the vain desire for resurrection.

This more humble mother senses Ana's loss and seems empathetic to Ana's desire to resurrect a loved one. She is a mother who knows suffering and does not barricade Ana from her children. Rather, she allows Ana to get close to her children and feel as though she is part of their family. The compassion Ana senses from the mother draws her closer to the boy and she begins to speak to him. She finds herself talking to him as if he were indeed her brother and they were both young children again:

> Ana se descubrió hablándole mudamente como si el niño fuera aquel otro que había crecido junto a ella. Le dijo palabras de ternura, sentados los dos en una parecita baja de ladrillos que daba a la calle. Rememoró una tarde de verano en la que ambos se habían alejado de la casa y una astilla del camino se le había clavado en el pie. Durante cuadras él la había llevado de regreso, a babuchas, como un salvador o San Cristóbal. Y su hermano recordaba con ella, y también el niño encimando las bandejitas de plástico. (183)

> Ana found herself speaking to him silently as if the boy was that other one who had grown up alongside her. She told him tender things, both of them seated on the low brick wall facing the street. She remembered a summer afternoon when they strayed from the house and a splinter stuck her foot. He carried her home for blocks, on his back, like a saviour or Saint Christo-

pher. And her brother remembered with her and so did the boy piling up the plastic trays.

It is during this interaction that a resurrection of her brother does indeed take place for Ana. As the narrator inserts, "And her brother remembered with her." Ana immerses herself further in her recollection of her brother and confesses to him her vain attempts at trying to remember him:

> Yo te seguía como una sombra, decía Ana, inclinándose hacia delante con la expresión de quien pretende hacer más íntima una charla, me fascinaban los juegos de varones que me estaban vedados, nunca me rechazaste, ni en la infancia ni en los años que siguieron. ¿Dónde te fuiste de muerto? Dónde se había ido ese niño, ese hombre robusto, de orejas que ya armonizaban con el rostro, risa estentórea y un poco petulante. Había intentado recuperarlo de muchas maneras sin conseguirlo, contemplo estos árboles de primavera que viste, cada día pronuncio las mismas palabras que compartimos, excusas o confortaciones que no nos traen de vuelta al ser ausente. (183–84)

> I followed you like a shadow, said Ana, leaning forward with the expression of someone trying to make the conversation more personal, fascinated by the boys' games that were forbidden me; you never rejected me, neither in childhood nor in the years that followed. Where did you go when you died? Where did that boy go, that strong man, with ears in harmony with his face, with that loud and somewhat arrogant laugh? I tried many ways of bringing him back to no avail; I contemplate these spring trees that you saw; every day I recite the same words that we shared, excuses or consolations that do not bring the missing person back to us.

By revisiting the memories associated with her brother, shared words, places, and experiences, Ana is able to restore her memory of him to life, but never his being. She is aware of this as she says "that do not bring the missing person back to us" but still harbors a hope of bringing him back, evidenced by her continuous responses to the young boy and his sister in the airport:

> El niño se desperezó alargando sus brazos en un movimiento de danza que era la de su hermano. Ella recogió la sonrisa con la prontitud que rescata una hoja cayendo en el aire. Estás de nuevo aquí, se conmovió, irrazonable y fugazmente aligerada, de nuevo aquí, en la intersección de tantas vidas, de tanta gente en este lugar ruidoso. Pero sabía que no, el niño sólo se parecía a su hermano, y la niña menor, que tenía los ojos cerrados de puro aburr-

imiento, no era ella. Ella era esa mujer ya grande que lamentaba la muerte de su hermano sentada con la espalda resentida sobre un asiento incómodo, en el interior de un aeropuerto donde el aire acondicionado no funcionaba, esperando horas su vuelo entre la fatiga y el hastío. Lo demás eran tretas que le hacía su nostalgia. (184)

The boy stretched out lengthening his arms in a dance movement that was her brother's. She picked up the smile with the readiness to catch a falling leaf in midair. You are here again, she was moved, irrationally and fleetingly uplifted, here again, in the intersection of so many lives, of so many people in this noisy place. But she knew that he wasn't, that the boy only resembled her brother, and the younger sister, whose eyes were closed out of pure boredom, was not her. She was that older woman sitting in an uncomfortable chair with a resentful back who mourned the death of her brother, in an airport where the air conditioning did not work, waiting for hours amid fatigue and annoyance for her flight. Everything else were tricks of her nostalgia.

The narrator assures the reader that this ruse is a figment of Ana's nostalgia. The "immateriality of death" causes Ana compulsively to repeat the loss of her brother. Upon bidding farewell to the little boy in the airport, Ana is deeply saddened:

Ana se despidió de su hermano niño. Te vas de nuevo, hermano, dijo en una queja, en un reproche. El niño la miró, los ojos oscuros, las orejas separadas del cráneo. Una sensación de ahogo la oprimió, el corazón desolado como ante una pérdida repetida. (185)

Ana said good-bye to her brother child. You are leaving again, brother, she complained, in disdain. The boy looked at her, his dark eyes, his ears sticking out. She felt suffocated, heartbroken by the repeated loss.

For Ana, this departure is the repeated experience of loss, likely to continue, and she watches on as the little girl also leaves. The girl follows distractedly and the mother calls out for her daughter: "La mujer se volvió, llamó con voz urgente: Ana, ¡Ana! Inmóvil en su asiento, Ana sintió un escalofrío, la certidumbre. La niña tomó la mano de su hermano. Y después de un segundo, ella fue" (185). [The woman turned around, called with urgency: Ana, Ana! Frozen in her seat, Ana felt a chill, the certainty. The girl took her brother's hand. And a moment later, she left.] Ana shivers as she hears her own name being called, directed to the young girl. She feels "la certidumbre," the certainty that the doubling of she and her brother within the airport has taken place.

The airport, this uncanny space of intersecting lives, arrivals and departures, has collapsed time and place, allowing Ana to reenter a "no longer living world" and relive the irrevocable past within the present.

"El encuentro," by its very title, reminds us of Lacan's interpretation of Aristotle's *tuché* (who uses it in his search for 'cause'). Lacan borrows *tuché* and defines it as *the encounter with the real*. Lacan states: "For what we have in psycho-analysis is an encounter, an essential encounter—an appointment to which we are always called with a real that eludes us" (53). Therefore, the "encounter" is also a missed encounter. For Ana, the real that eludes her is the trauma of loss, her brother's departure. In repetition of her memory of him, she encounters—meets him—and also misses the encounter, cannot physically encounter him. Lacan goes on to say, "The function of the *tuché*, of the real as encounter—the encounter in so far as it may be missed, in so far as it is essentially the missed encounter—first presented itself in the history of psycho-analysis in a form that was in itself already enough to arouse our attention, that of the trauma" (55). Ana's trauma is performed and she seems to be situated on the brink, between mourning and melancholia. Though she doubts that she is indeed seeing her double, her vacillation upon realizing that the young girl is also named Ana confirms her readiness to erase the distinction between past and present. She is possessed by her past, by her traumatic loss. A space of transference is cultivated, however, and Ana is able to act out her loss. This acting out is an essential aspect of working through trauma. As LaCapra states: "Possession by the past may never be fully overcome or transcended, and working through may at best enable some distance or critical perspective that is acquired with extreme difficulty and not achieved once and for all" (70). Therefore, I suggest that the mother is an empathic other who understands the importance of granting Ana a transferential or psychoanalytic space to act out her loss, to retrieve her memory. Her children, also, do not fear the "nonliving world" that Ana must reenter. Hence, "El encuentro" is a story that emits hope with regard to the healing of language and community.

Further expressing the importance of community, Gambaro's "El misterio de dar" criticizes society's indifference by asserting the need for social responsibility and consciousness with regard to class struggle in an era of economic crisis. In the postdictatorship era, Argentina has found itself in economic turmoil. In 1989, President Alfonsín was forced to step down when mobs began looting supermarkets amid the chaos of hyperinflation. Gambaro's "El misterio de dar" (The Mystery of Giving) exposes poverty in a country once relatively unaware of beggars, homeless, and *villas miseries* (ghettos).

Sra. Schneider, a retired middle-class woman, goes about her daily routine with obsessive caution: careful to walk slowly so as not to hyperventilate, careful to eat minimally so as not to have indigestion, careful about how she steps so as not to wear out her shoes, and careful with her money so as not to use her entire retirement check every month. Gambaro's Schneider reminds us of Nikolai Gogol's Akaky Akakyevich, who falls prey to the rules of the bureaucratic game in nineteenth-century St. Petersburg, Russia. Sra. Schneider follows the "rules of the game": "Estas eran las reglas del juego y si una las acataba se vivía de manera bastante agradable" (157). [These were the rules of the game and if one stuck to them, he lived rather well.] These are the keys to survival for the retired middle class experiencing economic crisis in Argentina. Unlike Akaky, however, Sra. Schneider learns "el misterio de dar," the secret of giving

On her way to the bank to pick up her pension, Sra. Schneider is shaken from her routine by a woman and a young boy who do not move along with the current of pedestrians along the sidewalk. The boy, with gauze and bandages over his left eye, strikes Sra. Schneider with the intense sadness emanating from his right eye: "la mirada del chico, más solitaria en su tristeza por el ojo ausente" (158). [the boy's gaze, more solitary in his sadness because of the missing eye.] As if something had possessed her, Sra. Schneider gives several coins to the mother and promises to give more after going to the bank. The boy's look, his helplessness, casts its power on Sra. Schneider, making her do something she normally would not. Once having left the mother and young boy, however, Sra. Schneider is surprised by the promise she made and contemplates changing her mind, doubting the intentions of the poor family:

> Bajo el vendaje estaría el ojo intacto y proyectaría una mirada distinta de la desolada, un ojo burlón, un poco cínico. Luchando entre la desconfianza y su promesa, la Sra. Schneider dudó por un instante, preguntándose si el vendaje no sería falso simple ardid para atraer su compasión. (160)

> Beneath the bandage was the intact eye and it projected a look unlike the desolate one, a teasing eye, a bit cynical. Torn between mistrust and her promise, Mrs. Schneider doubted for an instant, wondering whether the bandage was simply false trickery to win her compassion.

Sra. Schneider thinks that she is being taken advantage of and is afraid to trust her initial instincts. In her eyes, this poor family is not trustworthy. She does, however, promise to return with more money and cannot be unfaithful to the way she wishes to be seen through the eyes of others, especially through the boy's eye, which emanates sadness. She decides to confront the mother and confirm that the family is indeed in distress.

The mother shows Sra. Schneider hospital documents confirming the loss of the boy's eye and the cost to replace it with a glass one so the socket will not cave in. The mother does not plead with Sra. Schneider for money; but rather, she tells her that her children have not eaten and that they would like to go back to their town even if they cannot raise the money for the glass eye. Their trip to the city, where they are complete strangers, has made them feel more alone and desperate than ever. Sra. Schneider, surprised, finds herself handing over the largest bills of her pension and making the mother and children immensely happy:

> el alborozo incrédulo de quienes padecen en soledad y son impensablemente socorridos, que habían olvidado las razones primeras de ese viaje. En el rostro del niño la cuenca se cerraría de modo irrevocable, pero ya habría tiempo para dolerse. Hoy podrían comer, podrían regresar al pueblo que les resultaba familiar. (163–64)

> the unbelievable joy of those who live in solitude and are suddenly rescued, those who have forgotten the initial reason for that trip. The boy's eye socket would close irreparably, but there was still time to suffer. Today they would be able to eat; they would be able to return to their familiar village.

This gesture shakes Sra. Schneider from her fear of death's proximity and awakens her to the value of community and giving to those less fortunate—this gesture becomes the moment of seeing for Sra. Schneider. Unlike Akaky Akakyevich, who dies in utter solitude, Sra. Schneider experiences a "rebirth":

> la locura de conmover y conmoverse . . . algo extraño había pasado con el tiempo. Duraría, lo había temido tan próximo a la muerte y retornaba ya hacia ella, caudaloso e inmortal, como en su infancia. (164)

> The magic of reaching out and being moved . . . something strange happened over time. It would last, she had feared it so close to death and now it returned to her, strong and immortal, as in childhood.

The revelation Sra. Schneider has, that doing good for others makes life meaningful for her, echoes Bortnik's "El corazón de Celeste." Both

Celeste and Sra. Schneider feel empowered by acting upon what they know in their hearts to be good.

While criticizing the disparity among social classes, and especially the middle class's frugality, as well as the dehumanizing urban landscape that pushes individuals to the margin, Gambaro's story encourages compassion, solidarity, and community among the different social classes. Most importantly, the narrator encourages us to look to the margins, to difference, and to be critical of what we choose to see and recognize, encouraging us to question the established "rules of the game."

14. "Memoria sin tiempo." (Photo of the memorial in Córdoba, "Memoria sin tiempo," that Tununa Mercado refers to in "Piedras de Honda.") Photo courtesy of Liliana Felipe and Jesusa Rodríguez.

4

Tununa Mercado's Paper Cemeteries

Reading has unforseen effects and one of them is the urge to reconstruct lives according to the traces that a death notice, in its brevity, can weave together.
—Tununa Mercado

RECOGNIZED PRIMARILY AS A FEMINIST AUTHOR SINCE THE PUBLI-cation of *Celebrar a una mujer como a una Pascua* (Celebrate a Woman Like an Easter) (1967) and *Canon de alcoba* (Canon of the Bedroom) (1988), the journalist and translator Tununa Mercado writes in a style that is deeply marked by the experience of the two Argentine military dictatorships that drove her into exile along with her family: She lived in France from 1966 to 1970, during the military takeover led by Gen-eral Onganía; she then spent her second exile in Mexico from 1974 to 1986, returning to Argentina several years after democracy had been reinstated. Her subsequent publications, namely, *En estado de memoria* (*In a State of Memory*) (1990) and *La letra de lo mínimo* (The Letter of the Minimal) (1994), meditate on substantial issues of exile, marginal-ity, and memory. Mercado confirms her dedication to preserving mem-ory and working and writing through the aftermath of the Argentine Dirty War in the essays, vignettes, and journalistic entries that compose her most recent publication, *Narrar después* (Narrating Afterward) (2003). Taking into account that undoing traumatic entrapment is a process, one can read Mercado's short narrative, from *Canon de alcoba* to *Narrar después*, as progression through this process of working through or writing through trauma. Such is the reading of Mercado's work presented in this chapter.

Whereas neither Bortnik nor Gambaro explicitly defines the socio-historical reality to which her narrative attends, Mercado's writing is deeply autobiographical and anchored in the personal experiences she has endured. While Bortnik and Gambaro's works analyzed in the pre-vious two chapters are categorically defined within the genre of the short story, Mercado's work is more difficult to classify: her entries have been referred to as short stories, testimony, essays, vignettes, and journalistic accounts.

Additionally, scholars have been apprehensive about defining Mercado as the intended autobiographical narrator in these works. I read all of the works presented here as expressly narrated by Mercado, for she never once hints that it should be otherwise, and she identifies herself as the storyteller of her work. Moreover, after meeting and interviewing Tununa Mercado on several occasions, I have confirmed that she is narrating her own lived experiences. Though Mercado's narrative does not snugly fit the glove of *testimonio* as defined by John Beverley, for she is a professional writer and acts as her own interlocutor, her intentionality suggests an affinity with testimonial narrative in that she *needs* to narrate her experience.[1] It is Mercado who is undoing her own traumatic entrapment through writing, and it is she who progressively achieves successful mourning work—as defined by LaCapra—through literature.

Although, structurally, her collections of short entries are not easily defined, they complement the work of Gambaro and Bortnik in that they also attempt to open a space for considering the aftermath's traumatic nature: they too are defined as postcatastrophe literature that "reactivates the hope of providing an entrance into a traumatic experience that has seemingly been condemned to silence and oblivion" (Avelar 10). While offering such a space for the reader of the work, what distinguishes Mercado's writing is that she evidently is exploring the nature of what Avelar terms the literary crypt for herself. I will draw connections between Mercado's work and the short stories by Griselda Gambaro and Aída Bortnik.

Though Mercado is not as naturally equated with performance studies as Bortnik and Gambaro, who are easy identified as such for their work in film and theater, respectively, Mercado's writing is a performance: how an author uses literature to reconcile personal and national identity while mourning the catastrophes of the Dirty War. Borrowing from Diana Taylor's *The Archive and the Repertoire* (2003), I suggest that Mercado's work is an emblematic overlapping of the archive and the repertoire. While creating written documents that will form part of the archive of postcatastrophe literature, Mercado creates a personal account of working through trauma that is the enactment of her embodied experience. Indeed, as my reading will indicate, Mercado performs reconciliation and mourning within her body of writing. Her writing was, at its initiation, a "live" performance, one that she acted upon in order to externalize her experience upon return from exile. Though the initial performance was ephemeral and has vanished from the repertoire—it is now part of the archive—I suggest that the repertoire is performed continuously as Mercado's works are read. The reader becomes witness to Mercado's experiences and her metaexternalization of trauma. Furthermore, the first-person-singular *Yo* (I) narration contributes to potential transference and doubling—the reader may be drawn to identify with the narrative voice. The nonfictional and personal nature of Mercado's writing, coupled with its specific location in the process of mourning, brings the archive to life for the reader, while also deliberately pulling a traumatic history out of the archive. Incidentally Mercado attends to monuments, photos, and newspaper clippings—subjects typically relegated to the archive—and performs a dialogic relationship with them, so that they become alive for the reader, and thus performing her repertoire.

Mercado has identified herself as being in a *no-lugar,* a nonplace, and she works deliberately to blur boundaries and traditional modes of classification. A quotation from *En estado de memoria* is apropos to understanding Mercado's indeterminate position: "He percibido llamadas desde un espacio entre muro y alcoba, un entremedio que da cuenta de otra realidad" (80). [I have perceived a summons from within the spaces between the walls and the alcove, an intermediate space giving notice of another reality.][2] Her experience as a woman and as a writer who has experienced exile has deeply marked her work, both thematically and structurally: she claims to experience another reality. Mercado writes from a vicarious space, an "in-between" space that is very difficult to classify. Her criticism of power structures and imposed rules of taxonomy speaks to the importance of "interstitial space" asserted by Homi Bhabha in his introduction to *The Location of Culture:* "These 'in-between' spaces provide terrain for elaborating strategies of self-hood . . . that initiate new signs of identity, and innovative sites of collaboration, and contestation, in the act of defining the idea of society itself" (1). And indeed, Mercado's fragmented work, especially that of *En estado de memoria,* keeps her suspended in this "in-betweenness," where she is confronted with melancholy—immersed in the complexity of mourning, for she realizes that memory and forgetting are inextricably linked. Significantly, her statement that she is somewhere between the walls and the alcove also refers directly to the titles of her work: the *alcoba,* the alcove, whence she situates the stories that make up *Canon de alcoba,* and the *muro,* the wall, which she works to break down in the final entry of *En estado de memoria,* "El muro / The Wall." It is in this space where

she struggles with her personal and national identity, where her condition as exiled other leaves her in a constant state of contention, and
where her aphasia and obligation to write her experience wrestle with
one another. Indeed, it is "between walls and the alcove" that Mercado
elaborates "strategies of selfhood." Mercado embodies the raw aftermath, the ineffable that is at odds with the imposed construction of
identity, one that she has witnessed as it has produced consequences.

For Mercado, the end of exile, in its traditional sense—her return to
Argentina after years of living in Mexico—becomes the occasion for
producing her own literature of exile. Her first explicit articulation of
the experience of exile is found in *Canon de alcoba*. The brief text entitled "En que lugar" (In That Place) has been almost entirely overlooked
by scholars who have written about *Canon de alcoba*. The many articles
dedicated to the collection label it as either feminist or erotic, and
rightly so.[3] Indeed, *Canon de alcoba*, whose cover sports Fernando
Botero's "Venus," won the prestigious Boris Vian prize in 1988 as best
Argentine book. Mercado states in an interview with Gabriela Mora
that *Canon de alcoba* was given special attention for its erotic character
(79). It was probably not her intention virtually to hide the chapter entitled "Realidades" (Realities), where four texts devoted to the traumatic
reality of the time may be found: "En que lugar" explicitly defines the
condition of exile; "No saquemos el ojo" (We Won't Give Up) is dedicated to the death of Ortega Peña, who was assassinated in 1974 for
his criticism of the Peronist movement and denunciation of other assas-
sinations; "Asamblea" (Assembly) portrays the challenge of maintain-
ing democracy and allowing all voices to be heard; and "Fragmento de
una reflexión del general" offers a synthesis of Perón's contradictory
character. In fact, this somewhat subversive chapter is found at the center of *Canon de alcoba*, and the act of encompassing these works in what
she denotes as her "realities" is probably meant to draw attention to
them, "making visible the invisible" (Kaminsky 1993 25).

In her later publications, namely, *La letra de lo mínimo* and *Narrar
después*, Mercado pays reparation to these seemingly disappeared texts.
In the sarcastic and fictional posthumous note that opens *La letra de lo
mínimo*, she makes reference to *Canon de alcoba* and states that she is
remembered only for having written erotic literature. Undoubtedly,
Mercado winks at the reader, who should be well aware of the not-at-
all-erotic publication of *En estado de memoria*. Recognizing the need for
a careful reading of the lost chapter, "Realidades," Mercado explicates
the four brief entries in her essay "Explicaciones sobre política y
erótica" (Explanations about politics and erotica), published in *Narrar*

después (2003). Mercado seeks to restitute these lost texts, pulling them from the archive, admitting to their uncanny presence within the other works that compose *Canon de alcoba*. Evidently, as implied in the chapter title "Realidades," these were the realities she was living. This revisionary essay is found in the chapter "El no lugar" (*Narrar después*), where exile is a primary focus, for, in the aftermath, the *después*, Mercado realizes that these texts, the seedlings of the process of externalizing trauma and reconciling with her identity, have been lost. A reader of Mercado's oeuvre can see in retrospect that the spirit of Mercado's work has veered consistently in the direction of "Realidades" rather than toward the themes of erotica spanning *Canon de alcoba*. Mercado's repertoire, from the moment of return from exile, is inherently linked to a need to act out her lived experiences and reconcile with the haunting past.

"En que lugar" describes the experience of exile as both emptiness and growth—a deformity:

> Como si te cortaran el brazo y te creciera una buba, como si te arrancaran una uña y te creciera una joroba. Ni ojo por ojo, ni diente por diente, solo la deformación. . . . Andamos por el mundo como una raza nueva, como una especie que espera su clasificación . . . no ocupamos un espacio que naturalmente debiéramos ocupar entre los humanos, entre los propietarios, entre los ciudadanos, entre los nacionales, locales, regionales habitantes del mundo. (61)

> It's as if they cut off your arm and you grew a tumor; as if they tore out your fingernail and you grew a hunched back. Neither an eye for an eye nor a tooth for a tooth, just the deformity. . . . We wander the world like a new race, like a species waiting to be classified . . . we're not where we should naturally be among other humans, among proprietors, among citizens, among nationals, locals, regional inhabitants of the wold.

Upon writing "En que lugar," the sensation of being dislocated, *desterrado*, was such that Mercado felt as though she did not fit anywhere. This reaction calls to mind Bortnik's short story, "Ani-Nú y la belleza diferente," in which Ani-Nú is among the creatures that are too strange to fit in with the world. The less-than-300-word entry that makes up "En que lugar" is only a prelude to the many meditations on the position of exile found in Mercado's subsequent work. The act of inserting "Realidades" in *Canon de alcoba* is the initiation of Mercado's narration of her trauma. As the process of reexternalizing trauma often begins in fits and starts, and the narrator is uncertain of whether or not she will find an empathic listener or reader, Mercado is testing the waters for what soon becomes a trademark of her work: writing through trauma, which scholars such as Idelbar Avelar and Jean Franco have recognized in her work in *En estado de memoria*.

The return from exile ultimately forces Mercado to reconcile with the years she lived outside Argentina, to reconcile with her departure. The writing of *En estado de memoria* is a result of the overwhelming magnitude of the experience of return, one that obliges her to revisit the moment of her departure. Upon return, Mercado is confronted with the need to make sense of her life in exile and the years and events that transpired while she was away. Amy Kaminsky, in *After Exile*, offers a keen description of the task of return:

> The *desexiliados* must reconcile the different lives they lived elsewhere to the life that went on at home—reconcile not in the sense of making peace between the two but in bringing them together and making sense of them as necessary parts of a whole. People are bearers of place; the elsewheres the exiles lived became a little Latin American because of their presence; what they remembered marking home changed as a result of their leaving, of the dictatorships, and of the inevitable metamorphosis any complex living organism, whether individual or nation, undergoes with the passage of time. (37)

Mercado's "bringing them together and making sense of" her life in Mexico and the Argentina she did not physically witness is a process that begins in *Canon de alcoba* and evolves throughout her subsequent works: *En estado de memoria* is the descent into the crypt where Mercado lives her trauma and grapples with melancholy; *La letra de lo mínimo* is Mercado's deliberate practice of memory work, battling off melancholy through writing; *Narrar después* marks what Dominick LaCapra would define as successful memory work, in which Mercado has established a distance from her past that allows her to work toward social justice.

EN ESTADO DE MEMORIA

En estado de memoria, published two years after *Canon de alcoba*, has a tremendous impact on the way Mercado is perceived as an author. Previously given attention by feminist scholars, she suddenly receives acclaim as an author of the dictatorship period and is researched among other Southern Cone writers who wrestle with the contentious space of memory and forgetting in the aftermath of atrocity. Indeed, notable studies published by Idelbar Avelar and Jean Franco have included Tununa Mercado in what is now considered a canon of postdictatorship literature. The description on the back cover of *En estado de memoria* prefaces the book for the unsuspecting reader:

> Pero no es fácil escribir esos relatos, sobre todo si el que escribe está pegado a eso que está pasando, si lo vive y al mismo tiempo lo quiere trascender: se necesita tiempo y distancia para que la palabra sea consistente y no sólo autocompasiva o complaciente. Tal vez por eso no abundan relatos del drama argentino de la negra época de la dictadura; menos aún de algunos aspectos melancólicos, secretos, por ejemplo del exilio. Poco a poco; sin embargo, esos relatos se escriben; algunos, incluso, se escribieron, como éste, *En estado de memoria*. Tununa Mercado lo hizo, con una seriedad y profundidad como pocas veces se ha alcanzado en la literatura argentina.

> But it's not easy writing these stories, above all if the person who writes them has experienced them; if she lives precisely what she wishes to transcend. One needs time and distance in order for the written word to hold weight beyond being self-serving and therapeutic. Perhaps this is why there are not many stories about the Argentine drama during the dark era of the dictatorship; and less so about the melancholy, private aspects of exile. Little by little, however, these stories are being written, and some have been written as Tununa Mercado has, with severity and depth rarely achieved in Argentine letters.

While setting Mercado apart from other authors who have attempted to narrate traumatic experiences, this note also situates her among the most profound Argentine authors. Each entry in this collection deals with the complex and traumatic experience of coming to terms with one's personal and national identity upon return from exile. Her need to reconcile with that which she did not physically experience resembles the impossibility of representing the ungraspable nature of trauma, one that deceives consciousness.

As stated, these works are difficult to write because the author is intimately connected with what she is writing about and that which she wishes and needs to transcend. Trauma theorists debate whether victims have the ability to narrate or to know the life-jarring experience. Cathy Caruth notes in *Unclaimed Experience:* "Trauma seems to be much more than a pathology, or the simple illness of a wounded psyche: it is always the story of a wound that cries out, that addresses us in the attempt to tell us of a reality or truth that is not otherwise available" (4). Just as trauma "simultaneously defies and demands our witness" (Caruth 5), Mercado's return from exile both defies and demands her reconciliation with the historical reality of the Dirty War. In Bortnik's "Cuatro fotos" and "Crecé tranquilo," the articulation of trauma is riddled with elliptical spaces. In Gambaro's "Buscando la compañía del árbol," trauma has no chance of being communicated without the existence of an empathic other, and even then, Gambaro does not pretend to articulate the event: the protagonists of "El trastocamiento" and "El encuentro" live with their haunting pasts, never being able to speak of them. The entries that make up *En estado de memoria* do not claim to be easily written, but for Mercado, writing them was a necessary step in coming to terms with her reality. Only by sharing her experience can she inscribe herself once again among a community, and only by working through her trauma can she know herself and wish to be understood by others.

Evidently Mercado feels as if she belongs nowhere—though she did not experience the tortures of the Dirty War, her experience is one of immense isolation. The act of having left Argentina alienates her from the nation:

A los que se fueron, el país no podría acogerlos como hijos pródigos; no hay una práctica en ese sentido: nunca una persona, organismo o institución ha tenido la costumbre de considerar al ausente, al enajenado o al prófugo de la realidad, menos aún podría nadie hacer un gesto para entender la condición psicológica del desterrado; éste será siempre un inadaptado individual y social y su vida afectiva, como la del preso, el enfermo o el alienado, mantendrá sus circuitos lastimados y sus quemaduras no se restañarán con el simple retorno. Para el que regresa, el país no es continente y de nada valdrá que pretenda confundirse en las estructuras permanentes; no hay caja, no hay casa donde meterse. La sensación de extranjería asalta al regresante, es como si la persona estuviera envuelta, toda ella, su físico y su psiquis, de una membrana que la separa del mundo. (86)

For those who fled, the country could not reabsorb them as if they were prodigal sons and daughters; there is no precept in this sense: no person, organism, or institution has ever taken into account people who have been absent, estranged, or fugitive from reality, and much less could anyone begin to understand the psychological condition of the exile; they will always be maladjusted, asocial individuals whose emotional lives, like those of prisoners, the ill, or the alienated, will preserve their damaged circuitry, and their wounds will not be stanched upon their simple return. For those who return, the country is not an open container, and it is futile for them to try to lose themselves within the existing structures; there are no cubby holes to slip into, no houses in which to hide. The sense of foreignness hurls itself at the returning exile; it is as if the entire person, their body and psyche, were swaddled in a membrane separating them from the world.

It is precisely this "membrane," separating Mercado from the world, that she must remove in order to become part of a community once again. This breakdown of community, of belonging, of language echoes the difficulty of feeling a sense of belonging that torture victims experience.[4]

Though Mercado tries to recall happy moments experienced in exile, she is inundated with a sense of melancholy: "La melancolía lleva la delantera, nada se sustrae a la melancolía de un recuerdo gris, aunque muy intenso" (20). [A sense of melancholy predominates; nothing escapes the melancholy feeling of this gray, albeit intense, memory.] She tackles the myth that those who went into exile had it easy and describes the incessant nightmares that assaulted her. Her return to Argentina is an awakening of the trauma that pursued her in an unconscious state. As the narration of trauma is often subject to a belatedness, for trauma cannot be spoken of at the moment of its occurrence, the years she spent in exile suddenly overwhelm her when she returns to Buenos Aires. She looks in the mirror and finds she has aged, seemingly twice as much as those who remained in Argentina. Though in exile, and seemingly protected from the horrors of the Dirty War, she still must bear the weight of them. As soon as she returns home, she becomes witness to many things she was not physically present to experience. Though the concept of the "transgenerational phantom" does not apply here, since this trauma is not being passed down unconsciously from an older generation, her experience speaks to a "transnational phantom," one that she can only become aware of when she crosses the border into Argentina and sees her reflection. Unconsciously, the tyranny has been transmitted. Her claims that time stood still while living in exile speak to Freud's analysis of the incubation period, when trauma remains dormant between the moment of the traumatic event, Mercado's departure, and the awareness of the event, her return:[5]

> Los años no corrían en ese largo paréntesis. Tal vez esta dislocadura fuera consecuencia, o síntoma paralelo, de una desestructuración del exilio mismo, pero nadie se permitía esas cuestiones y a nadie se le ocurría poner en hora el reloj biológico del destierro. El tema fue propuesto por mí al psicólogo que me atendió cuando los dorados atacaron mi organismo; le dije que me desesperaba no cumplir años, que tenía la descabellada idea de que el tiempo no transcurría. (44)

> The years ceased to roll along during that long parenthesis. Perhaps this dislocation was a consequence, or a parallel symptom, of a destructuralization of exile itself, but no one ventured to analyze such questions, nor did anyone attempt to set their "biological clock-in-exile." I brought the subject up with my psychologist, the one who treated me when my throat was attacked

by golden blisters; I told him I was upset about missing my birthdays, that I had this crazy idea that time was standing still. (48)

When she looks at herself in the mirror, finding that she has aged considerably, her face bears an ashen complexion and her whole body seems to be covered in a fine gray dust. She is a vessel harboring the phantoms of the disappeared:

> En el primer viaje a Buenos Aires en 1984, de puro carácter exploratorio e intensamente cargado de negatividad, me vi a mí misma mirándome en el espejo y descubriendo, en un instante, en la piel, los ojos, las comisuras, el ciclón de esos diez años; y no eran arrugas, ni otros signos de decrepitud, era otra cosa, un polvo fino y gris, y por lo mismo macabro, que cubría como si fuera una pátina la totalidad de mi figura. Mi imagen había adquirido el tono sepia de las viejas fotografías, un rubor ceniciento. Podría decir que hasta ese momento revelador incluso yo tenía la sensación de que la gente había envejecido mucho en la Argentina y que quienes nos habíamos ido, por el contrario, habíamos permanecido iguales, situados en ese paréntesis del no transcurso. (44–45)

> On my first trip to Buenos Aires in 1984, purely out of curiosity and highly charged with negativity, I found myself examining my own face in the mirror and discovering, all in an instant, in my skin, my eyes, the corners of my mouth, the cyclone of those ten years; and it was not the discovery of wrinkles, or other signs of decrepitude: it was something else, a fine gray powder, rather macabre, like a patina, that covered the totality of my being. My image had acquired the sepia tone of old photographs, an ashen glow. I would say that, until the revealing moment, I shared the view and the sensation that the people of Argentina had aged very much while those who had left, in contrast, had remained the same, suspended in that parenthesis of impotence.

The impact of return, the collision of the experience of exile and that of the losses suffered, is an awakening for Mercado, a rude awakening that impels her to write.

She tells in an interview with Gabriela Mora that she began writing *En estado de memoria* upon her return to Argentina, feeling as though she was drowning. Her husband, the renowned Latin American literary critic Noé Jitrik, encouraged her to write and she did: "Me levanté como una autómata y me senté frente a la máquina de escribir. Los textos fueron saliendo tal como han quedado en el libro, desde el primero, 'La enfermedad,' hasta el último, 'El muro,' sobre el que escribo y en el que me disuelvo" (78). [I got up like an automaton and sat down in front of the typewriter. The texts came out just as they are in the book, from the very first one, 'The Illness,' to the last one, 'The Wall,' about which I write and in which I dissolve.] Unlike *Canon de alcoba*, this collection is not broken down into chapters. All sixteen entries encompass what Mercado denotes as being in a "state of memory." Borrowing from Primo Levi's assertion that Holocaust victims can be separated into two categories, "the drowned and the saved," I suggest that it is Mercado's will to articulate her experience that saves her from drowning when she is overwhelmed by her on return to Argentina.

She embodies Fernando Reati's assertion that the postdictatorship years, the 1990s, are ripe with the conflict between the will to remember and the attempt to forget. Mercado finds herself cast within the traumatic experience, living the tense space of "en estado de memoria":

Hay un largo periodo en los retornos, el de la evocación, pautado por señales que se producen a cada paso, como si una masa de significaciones hubiese estado a la espera de quien la excitara para desencadenarse, irrefrenable. Se sale a la calle *en estado de memoria*, ya sea que se la bloquee o se la deje en libertad de prenderse a los datos de la realidad. (86–87)

Returning involves a long period, that of evocation, marked by signs that appear at every turn, as if a mass of meanings were just waiting for someone to stumble into them and to set off an irrepressible, explosive, chain reaction. One steps into the street in a state of memory, either having blocked memory out or having left it at liberty to grasp the substance of reality. (103)

This tension of either blocking out or letting in the historical reality of the postwar period becomes impetus for Mercado's repertoire, repeatedly resurfacing throughout her work. Mercado explains the complexity of understanding the traumatic experience, the ineffable, and her difficulty of consciously coming to terms with the reality. She narrates her firsthand experience in the final entry, "El muro" (The Wall). Since the Argentina she has returned to is now haunted, Mercado's psyche resists recognizing the once-familiar places she strolls through upon return. After several months of taking daily walks on the same blocks, she suddenly realizes—after her companion notes a familiar aroma from a restaurant—that she has been circling her old "haunts": the building where she worked, the restaurant where she lunched, the home she often visited of the political journalist par excellence, Rodolfo Walsh, who was disappeared the day after the publication of his "Carta abierta a la junta militar" (Open Letter to the Military Regime) in 1977.

Mercado explicitly grapples with the return to Argentina after years of exile and the difficulty of revisiting memories and places that were so much a part of her life before the Dirty War. She confesses that coming to terms with the past defies her consciousness:

> Quiere decir, pensé que la material se había volatizado para mí durante semanas, que un sector del universo, de la historia, de la conciencia, había dejado de funcionar con todos sus atributos de realidad, que había sido víctima de una afasia selectiva y, además, reiterada, porque no se había producido una sola e inocente vez la borratina sino cada día. (120)

> This meant, I reasoned, that the elements had become volatile for me over those last few weeks, that a sector of the universe, of history itself, of consciousness, had stopped functioning with all of its reality-based attributes, that I had fallen victim to a selective and repeated aphasia because the erasure had not been produced on one single and innocent occasion but, rather, every day.

She struggles with either visiting or avoiding these haunted places. Finally, she decides that she must face them and she sets out for the home she lived in before exile. At first she cannot bring herself to enter. Home, the most symbolic of places to confront loss during her process of reconciliation, is the most difficult, the most loaded with conflict, as it reminds her of her vulnerability: this space called "home" is a precarious one, as affirmed by the experience of the dictatorships. Mercado articulates precisely what Reati describes as the crux of the aftermath. She can continue to avoid her old home, her old familiar zone, the places she worked and lunched, but she chooses instead to enter the crypt and confront the phantoms.

Although she decides to take the step, no longer fleeing "the abyss," she finds herself unable to enter her old home. She is overwhelmed with anxiety and turns back:

> Con más convicción que nunca decidí darme la tarea de no practicar ninguna forma de huída, de no eludir el foso, ni franquearlo con malas artes y, sobre todo, a partir de ese momento, desconfié de la lucidez y de la vigilia. Intenté pasar por la última casa que habíamos habitado, un edificio de departamentos con un ancho corredor en planta baja que terminaba en un jardín encerrado y rumoroso. Allí el fragmento de la realidad tenía una contundencia insoslayable; pero no se dejaba agarrar por otras razones, traumáticas en línea directa: quería pasar por mi antigua casa y cuando llegaba a la esquina de esa calle y me iba acercando, me daba un ataque de pánico,

curiosamente no en el pecho, sino en la espalda, y me regresaba sin haber podido cumplir la misión. (121)

With more conviction than ever I set myself to the task of no longer fleeing from anything, no longer avoiding the abyss, nor passing over it through cunning, and, above all, from that moment on, I no longer trusted lucidity or wakefulness. I tried to visit the last house we had lived in, an apartment building with a wide corridor on the ground floor that ended in an enclosed murmur-filled garden. There, the fragment of reality had inescapable force; but I could not grapple with it for other decidedly traumatic reasons: I wanted to visit my old house, but just as I was arriving at the corner of the street, just drawing near, I experienced a terrible sense of panic, not in the chest, curiously enough, but in the back, and I returned home without having been able to carry out my mission.

Mercado's anxiety upon facing the once-familiar places rings of Tulio Halperín Donghi's assertion that one's relationship with his or her own country after the dictatorship can never be the same after witnessing death in those familiar places. Mercado's relationship with Argentina, with her old house, can never be as it once was. Finally one morning she takes a taxi to the front entrance and crosses the threshold. Her experience, however, is not one of reconnection. She is overwhelmed by a phantasmal flashback ("phantasmal" because the event she experiences never happened to her before): it is a flashback of that which she most feared, that which forced her to go into exile. When she arrives at her home, three men begin chasing her. Just as she thinks she has escaped them and sneaks back into the taxicab, they grab her from behind. The nightmare of being caught by the Triple A pursues her even in the aftermath. Why does Mercado suffer in such a real way? Does she feel guilty for having survived? Does she unconsciously desire to embody the experience of being "disappeared"? Perhaps her unconscious drives her to fulfill this rite in order to move her closer to the community she wishes to be a part of; perhaps only by suffering in such a visceral way can she be empathetic to her compatriots who were not fortunate enough to live safely in exile. The manifestation of her utmost fear is an encounter with the real that Mercado must perform in order to understand the traumatic reality of the Dirty War.

Facing her new apartment, where she feels less than "at home," is a solid wall that she observes at different times of day, watching its tone change according to the intensity of the Sun. This wall is the screen onto which Mercado projects the representation of the traumatic experience. After the traumatic "encounter" at her old house, the wall reflects a blinding glare and heat so intolerable that she is forced to close the shutters and retreat to a cooler part of her apartment, hiding from her unconscious. The wall is the barrier, the "membrane," the obstacle preventing Mercado from returning to Argentina, from externalizing her losses and coming to terms with her "home." Writing is her means of breaking down or dissolving this barrier, *el muro*. When she finally takes up her pen and starts writing "con caracteres pequeños, caligrafía desgarbada, y desde el ángulo superior izquierdo" (124) [in small, awkward letters, in the upper-left-hand corner], the wall begins to fall away:

> Y el muro, sobrecargado de una violenta energía, traspasado por su foso y dominado por un prolongado sitio, se fue cayendo, literalmente, sobre la línea recta de su base; no se desmoronó arrojando cascotes como edificio de terremoto, sino que se filtró sobre su línea fundante, como un papel que se desliza vertical en una ranura. (124–25)

> And the wall, overloaded by a violent energy, pierced and racked by graffiti, exposed to an inclemency heretofor unknown, constrained by the chasm and dominated by a prolonged siege, began to crumble, literally, upon the straight line at its base; it did not collapse and fling rubble in all directions, as a building might during an earthquake, but, rather, it slid down into the line at its very foundation, like a sheet of paper sliding vertically into a slot.

The wall does not crash down as if struck by an earthquake. Rather, it filters down onto its foundations. As trauma is the foundational makeup of this wall; it is upon working through its base that the wall weakens and disintegrates.

Traumatic entrapment is not undone instantly, but through a process. Idelbar Avelar astutely recognizes Mercado's work as one that proves the potential to write trauma—the author's finding that only through writing can she engage with her entrapment and work toward fostering a relationship with a community; only by externalizing her fears and reconciling with the Argentina she fled can she break down the barriers that isolate her and allow her to cross thresholds into her past—reconnecting with the country to which she has returned:

> *En estado de memoria* is thus a prolegomenon to postdictatorial writing in that it narrates the conditions of possibility for writing after a catastrophe. The true story has not been told. Following the protagonist's compelling refusal of all substitutive, compensatory mechanisms, and her decision not to elude the abyss of depression and melancholia, the final scene announces

writing as the locus where the confrontation with the pathology can truly take place beyond the mere identification of the symptom, in a movement that is not simply a dive into the subject's interiority but a decisive reconnection with the outside. What might at first appear to be a highly introspective text ends with a gesture toward an unnamed, unknown outside that represents the only possibility of activating subjective memory along with a space of intervention in the polis. (228)

Thus, Mercado's personal struggle to externalize her experience is that which fosters a relationship with community. Seemingly, this is an anachronistic collection of entries, for, as evidenced by the texts preceding "El muro," Mercado has already been working/writing through the wall. Similarly to Bortnik in the story "¿Te acordás?" she decides to stop holding up the building, the wall that prevents her from letting in her history and the world with its suffering. "El muro" is the culmination of the preceding texts: having successfully worked through the many barriers they present, Mercado is able to articulate her traumatic experience of return and reconciliation through writing. Likewise, as a result of the repetitive nature of traumatic memories, one may read *En estado de memoria* as a cyclical work and return to the beginning once again. Or, after one has read *La letra de lo mínimo* and *Narrar después*, *En estado de memoria* may be read as a precursor to another stage in the mourning process.

The first entry of *En estado de memoria*, entitled "La enfermedad" (The Illness), is an allegory of the penetratingly harsh reality of the injustices sown on Argentine soil, but also as the pinnacle of Mercado's anguish—feeling helpless in the face of the Argentine national reality. She draws the reader directly into the realm of her memory, directly into the waiting room of a psychiatric clinic, where a man named Cindal bursts in screaming with agony for help. "El aullido tenía paralizada a la gente de la antesala que habíamos acudido por problemas menores si los comparaba con la situación terminal de Cindal" (7). [The patients, assembled in the waiting room for problems that were quite minor compared to Cindal's terminal situation, were frozen, gripped by his shrieks and howls.] Cindal is identified as an atypical patient, one whose condition is more severe than that of the other patients at the clinic. His situation is terminal, a bleak prognosis with no possible cure. Cindal is a pest because he has shown up without an appointment: "La secretaria . . . no sabía cómo manejar este caso fuera de todo orden, sin turnos, sin citas previas, que irrumpía sin haberse anticipado por teléfono" (7). [The receptionist . . . had no idea how to deal with the unusual case that had barged into the office with no prior phone call, no appointment, and no previous visits.] The controlling and dehumanizing system does not know how to handle the unexpected, Cindal, and immediately treats him as a threat, trying to get rid of him rather than accommodate him.

Cindal interrupts the authoritarian control of the clinic. He is noisy and demands attention, a nuisance because he speaks openly about his ulcer, about the pain he suffers. In response, the psychiatrist treats Cindal with "analytical silence" so that he will toughen up and deal with his reality on his own. The psychiatrist is master of silence:

> Ya en el consultorio, no respondió a ninguna de nuestras preguntas y se quedó en silencio; tengo entendido que con el tiempo se ha ido perfeccionando ese silencio analítico hasta ser de ultratumba para quienes buscan respuestas inmediatas a su desesperación. Cindal se ahorcó esa misma noche. (8)

> The psychiatrist, once in his office, maintained a strict silence that would not respond to a single one of our questions; I understand that over time psychiatrists have perfected this analytical, beyond-the-grave silence insofar as anyone desperate for immediate answers is concerned. Cindal hanged himself that very night.

Since Cindal cannot control or hide his desperation, the psychiatrist and the authoritarian system shun him, isolating him with his suffering. Such neglect and refusal to treat him leave Cindal alone to be tortured by his pain. The absence of an empathic other, as for the young female protagonist of Gambaro's "Buscando la compañía del árbol," leaves Cindal with no potential to narrate his suffering. In contrast to Gambaro's story, in which an empathic other does eventually approach the young woman who is in pain to lessen her suffering, no one pays Cindal any attention and his desperation is such that he commits suicide later that night.

Even his pleading with the other patients in the waiting room (including the narrator) does not convince anyone to sacrifice a few minutes of his or her appointment so Cindal can seek help: "la hora era inviolable" (7). [the hour was sacred.] The rigid control imposed in the clinic has influenced the witnesses, the other patients, who remain as spectators to Cindal's suffering and as accomplices to his isolation and suicide. The spectators—those who repress any potential protest and who accept the "analytical silence" imposed by the psychiatrists—justify Cindal's suicide so as not bear any guilt or responsibility for their passivity:

A gente así, que sufre con tanta convicción—se dijo después que Cindal se colgó de su cuerda—hay que dejarla, no se puede hacer nada; y cuando gente así busca su propia muerte y la halla, se suele pensar que encontró la paz, que suavemente se deslizó a otra cosa y que a fin de cuentas ha cesado de sufrir. A Cindal lo dejaron morir porque se pensó que eso era lo que quería y que tarde o temprano iba a encontrarlo. (8)

People like that who suffer with such conviction—this was said after Cindal had hung himself from a rope—must be left alone, nothing can be done for them; and when such people seek and find their own death, it is commonly agreed that they have found peace, that the have gently slipped away, and that, in the end, they have ceased to suffer. Cindal was left to die because it was thought that death was what he really wanted and that sooner or later he was going to have his way.

The synthesis of this ideology echoes the oft-repeated phrase when speaking about the *desaparecidos*, "Por algo será," it happened for some reason, placing blame on the victim for having done something wrong. Bortnik, Gambaro, and Mercado make a point to note the compliance of the witnesses during Argentina's Dirty War. As Diana Taylor states in *Disappearing Acts*, Argentines feared for their lives: "As the military reiterated constantly, the population was either supportive of their mission, or their next target" (124). Cindal represents the injustice and profound alienation experienced by victims of repression and the breakdown of language that results from censorship and fear instilled by the authoritarian regime.

Mercado differentiates between her own conduct and Cindal's. Whereas he could not help but plead for his life with no trace of pride or shame, Mercado silences and hides her anguish:

Yo, en cambio, postergo de una manera obstinada cualquier afloramiento de la angustia, en gran parte por buena educación, para no arruinarle la fiesta a nadie, escondiendo mediante artimañas altos picos de aflicción que me asaltan. (9)

I, on the other hand, obstinately postpone any outburst of anguish, partly due to my good upbringing, not wishing to ruin anyone else's party, employing any number of stratagems in an effort to disguise the agonizing peaks of the affliction that assaults me.

Such "stratagems" do not allow the narrator's own anguish to surface. The truth, her affliction, is always hidden because she is obsessed with not upsetting anyone while attending group therapy sessions. She yearns for the acceptance of the collective. The narrator resolves to hide in the group's laughter and tears, never developing her own voice, and thus implicating the collective in the breakdown of language and communication—which become prey to censorship and authoritarian threats.

In "La enfermedad," similarly to Ana María Shua's *Soy paciente* (*Patient*) (1980), the state convinces people that they are ill and they begin valuing their illnesses: "Esta suposición de que yo podía tener una existencia como caso me tranquilizó: mi salud o mi enfermedad mentales cobraron un carácter singular" (10). [The idea that I might have an existence as a *case* calmed me down a bit: my health, or my mental illness, had assumed a singular character.] The mere fact that the psychologist acknowledges the narrator calms her and gives her the illusion of having her own identity, the illusion that there is a place for her in society: "En la terapia nunca dejaba de inculcársenos que estábamos allí como enfermos mentales" (10). [And it was not inappropriate to speak of a mental illness since it was constantly impressed upon us during our therapy sessions that we were there as mental patients.] Repeatedly referring to the patient as mentally ill helps her accept her new identity and seek refuge within it. While disempowering her, by deeming her imperfect and unhealthy, and silencing her voice and mind, such an analysis also empowers her to feel guilt-free, thus enabling her to be a passive witness without an opinion, without criticism, blinding her to her own reality. The protagonist of Shua's novel, although never given a definitive prognosis, after being hospitalized against his will eventually resigns himself to remaining in the Sala de Hombres (Men's Ward), finding relief in no longer having to question his surroundings or trying to escape from them. He joins in song with the other patients: *"El que entra en esta sala / ya no se quiere ir, / quédate con nosotros / que te vas a divertir. / Catéter por aquí, / y plasma por allá, / el que entra en esta sala / no sale nunca más"* (134). [He who enters this room / won't want to leave, / stay with us / you'll have fun. / Catheter over here, / and plasma over there / he who enters this room / will never leave again.]

Although the narrator of "La enfermedad" is conscious of the lie that is being perpetuated within society, she does not question it or denounce it. Rather, she accepts her diagnosis and cedes to the powers that be. While supposedly trying to cure her own relentless anguish, she attends several group therapy sessions, even one in which the patients are given hallucinogens. In the aftermath, however, Cindal's screams continue to haunt her, and she is driven to write about him while also confessing her own passivity, both as spectator and as ghostwriter. The last line of Gambaro's play *Atando cabos* resonates here: "¡El silencio grita!" [Silence screams!] Mercado can no longer repress the memory of Cindal or continue to hide among the collective experience: "A Cindal, cuyo nombre me viene con regularidad a la memoria siempre acentuado en la letra *i*, e cuyo gesto de doblarse se me reitera en sucesivas evocaciones" (8). [Cindal, whose name returns to me with regularity, always with the stress on the letter *i*, whose twisted posture appears over and over.] The traumatic repetition of the memory of Cindal impels Mercado to narrate "La enfermedad" so as not to drown in the boundless grief that overwhelms her.

Thus, *En estado de memoria* commences with haunting, with Mercado's confession and criticism of society's complicity, and with a pledge to develop her own voice. While living in exile in Mexico, Mercado begins to understand the need for an empathic other. She meets Pedro, who spends a lot of time with the exile community. He is not Argentine, Chilean, Uruguayan, or Guatemalan as the others are. Rather, Pedro went to Mexico as a child refugee from the Spanish civil war. While fleeing Franco's soldiers and bombs, he was separated from his parents. Although they were eventually reunited, the trauma of the separation persisted and Pedro is caught in the repetition of the moment:

> Pero el aparente final feliz, la reunión familiar, no logró de todos modos y contra cualquier previsión, mitigar los daños en el niño, ni en el padre, ni, sobre todo, en la madre. Pedro se pasó la vida esperando a su madre que había ido por el agua y ella buscando a su hijo que siguió al sur. (71)

> However, the apparent happy ending with the family reunited was not such a complete and unconditional success in mitigating the damage to the child, or to the father, or, moreover, to the mother. Pedro spent the rest of his life waiting for his mother, who had left him to go in search of water, and she continued to search for her son, who had gone on without her toward the south.

Pedro gravitates toward the new exile community in Mexico, receptive and empathetic to his exile experience, and Mercado realizes that she too is looking for solace. She finds herself drawn to the homes of Diego Rivera and Frida Kahlo, as well as repeatedly to the exiled home of Leon Trotsky and his wife, Natalia Sedova:

> No sé por qué habré repetido tantas veces ese "paseo" por su jardín y sus recámaras, hasta concluir en el taller de Frida y en el horrible retrato de Stalin que permanece en su caballete, si no fue también para buscar las trazas de mi fundación, por así decirlo: guerra de España, guerra mundial, nazismo, campos de concentración, y también stalinismo, policías secretas, confe-

siones abyectas, derrotas y esperanzas y ese halo de aquellas décadas en las que nací y crecí. Cada vez que yo entraba en esas casas, la primera de la calle Viena, la segunda de la calle de Allende, las dos en Coyoacán, sentía que ingresaba en una muy lejana e imaginaria casa "paterna" que, saltando las décadas, transmigraba para cobijarme. (76)

I do not know why I repeated that "circuit" through the garden and the bed-rooms so often, ending up in Frida's studio and in the presence of that hor-rible portrait of Stalin that remains on the easel, were it not to find traces of my own formation: war in Spain, world war, Nazism, concentration camps, Stalinism, secret police, abject confessions, defeats and hopes, and that halo of those decades in which I was born and grew up. Every time I entered those houses, the first on Vienna Street, the second on Allende Street, both in Coyoacán, I felt that I was entering a very distant and imaginary "pater-nal" house that, leaping decades, had transmigrated to offer me shelter.

Mercado returns to these homes because they foster a sense of belong-ing she is unable to find elsewhere, one that ties her identity as exile to the many other storms of fascism in the twentieth century. Her expe-rience links her to Pedro, to Trotsky, to Rivera and Kahlo. As Caruth states in *Unclaimed Experience:* "History, like trauma, is never simply one's own, that history is precisely the way we are implicated in each other's traumas" (24). Mercado's assertion here will become even more apparent in *Narrar después.*

She further meditates on the meaning of "home" and her relation to houses in the following entry, appropriately entitled "Casas" (Houses). She finds herself living a totally provisional existence where nothing pertains to her, and she is disconnected from her surroundings:

No aparecía en mí la voluntad de hacerme de una casa o, mejor dicho, de hacer mía la casa que ocupaba. Este deseo obliterado causaba la sensación de vivir, desde siempre, en una provisoriedad total, sin arraigo a los sitios, sin fijación en los objetos, desposeída de esa lógica de la apropriación común a los humanos por razones que no lograba entender.

I seemed to lack the drive necessary for adapting to a new home or, more accurately, for accepting the house I was living in as my home. For as long as I can remember and for reasons I could not understand, this obliterated desire rendered the sensation of being alive totally provisional, without roots, without fixation to objects, dispossessed of the logic of appropriation that is common to human beings.

Even though she would physically go through the motions of making herself "at home," she could not truly develop a sense of belonging.

Por más que me esforzara en quedarme en lugares en los que me tocaba vivir, siempre me estaba yendo; había un plazo interno de partida que no me dejaba margen para instalarme; este plaza era permanentemente prorrogado, puesto que en muchos sitios me quedaba largo tiempo, y no significaba la inacción: llegaba, me ubicaba con facilidad; no pasaban unas horas y yo ya estaba acomodando las mesas, las sillas, poniendo algo en las paredes, en los cajones, en los estantes, pero pese a esa adecuación instantánea, algo misterioso me impedía sentir que *allí estaba*, que ese espacio en orden era mi casa. (77)

As much as I tried to stay put in the places where I was compelled to live, I was forever on the move; there was an internal time limit that left me no margin for settling myself into any one place; this time limit was always being deferred, given that I remained in many places for long periods of time, but this did not imply inaction: I would arrive, I would orient myself with ease; within hours of my arrival I would already be arranging the tables, the chairs, putting things on the walls, in the drawers, the shelves, but despite this instantaneous settling in, something mysterious still prevented my feeling that *I was there*, that the ordered space was really my home.

The repeated experience of exile, of in-betweenness, and Mercado's association with the innumerable exiles and migrations caused by political unrest have branded upon her the vicarious nature of physical and material attachments.

Upon preparing to return to Argentina and acquiring a new "home," Mercado is haunted by all that has transpired during her departure, the long parenthesis that was her experience of exile. She wishes for the flight to continue past Argentina and never touch down. When it is time for her to face her new "home" she is unsettled by an accumulating notion of haunting:

Pero llegó el momento en que la casa forjada en la fantasía cobró realidad. La casa ya estaba, era esta vez un departamento que habríamos de ocupar a nuestro regreso a la Argentina, había sido adquirida, se salía de sueño y del proyecto. No obstante, la soñé y una fuerza recurrente volví a configurar en mi pesadilla la reiterada estructura modular: las habitaciones inexploradas sólo contenían espanto y ese espanto crecía a medida que se acercaba el momento de habitarlas. (79–80)

But the moment arrived when the house forged in my fantasy gave way to reality. The house was there waiting for us, an apartment this time, already acquired for our occupancy upon our arrival in Argentina, and thus it departed from my dreams and projections. Even so, I still dreamed of the house, and a recurring force shaped the reiterated modular structure in my nightmare: the unexplored rooms only contained terror, and this terror increased as the moment of our moving into them drew near.

Ultimately, Mercado finds herself looking outward and identifying with those on the margin of society, those who are homeless, and she fixates on the *linyeras*, the vagabonds, at the park outside her window. Particularly, she is drawn to Andrés, who spends hours bent over his notebook and writing feverishly. She observes him for over a month, wonders about his welfare during bouts of inclement weather, and finally approaches him to find that he is working to solve mathematical equations, taking advantage of his situation on the margins of society to dedicate himself to these problems that have been with him for years. Andrés's choice to live in the park puzzles Mercado and she questions whether her own sense of marginality is a choice or an identity imposed upon her:

> No sabía cuál era mi intemperie y no podía saber por lo tanto cuál era la suya y, además, esa inquietud por su presunta decisión de intemperie se ofrecía con tanta naturalidad para la escritura que entré a sospechar de ella, no fuera a ser ahora que convirtiera la intemperie inclemente del hombre en un tema literario, cuando mi decisión había sido hacer de este relato una catarsis despojada de toda vanidad. (103–4)

> I did not know what my own situation of exposure was, and I could not know, therefore, what his was either, and, furthermore, this interest in his presumed decision to live exposed to the elements was offered to me so aptly for transference onto paper that I became suspicious, not wanting to convert the exposure of the man into a literary theme when my decision had originally been to use the narrative as catharsis devoid of all vanity.

She realizes that it is her own state of *intemperie*, of exposure, that has been converted into a literary subject. Fittingly, "Intemperie" (Exposure) precedes the final story, "El muro," where Mercado concludes that she must write her own status as outsider in order to dissolve the immense wall surrounding her life and inscribe herself within the community in which she longs to be a part.

LA LETRA DE LO MÍNIMO

Mercado's *La letra de lo mínimo* (1994) has received little attention in the shadow of *En estado de memoria*. Perhaps this will soon change as it was reprinted by Beatriz Viterbo in 2003. Indeed, it is in *La letra de lo mínimo* that Mercado recapitulates her thoughts on feminism, eroticism, sexuality, memory, and the act of writing. *La letra de lo mínimo* is a deeply philosophical collection of entries spanning the issues that have been dominant in her previous publications. Whereas the reader of *En estado de memoria* finds a narrator who is literally entrenched in a "state of memory," walking the streets of Buenos Aires draped in her memories, seeking solace, *La letra de lo mínimo* offers the reader a Mercado who has surpassed the obstacle of the wall—the entrapment so evident in *En estado de memoria* has loosened its grip upon her. While the palpable trauma of *En estado de memoria* may be transmitted to the reader, Mercado has established some distance from the crypt in *La letra de lo mínimo*, thus making for a less emotionally charged reading experience than its precursor. Hence, I suggest that Mercado has successfully undone her traumatic entrapment via the mourning work exercised in *En estado de memoria*.

La letra de lo mínimo begins with the fictional posthumous epitaph mentioned previously—Mercado's writing from the crypt. The note is humorous and symbolically marks Mercado's ability to distinguish between the events of her past and the present, the necessary step of removing oneself from the melancholic cycle of traumatic repetition. In this note, Mercado is remembered only for her erotic literature: "Y sólo se tiene noticia de un volumen de textos. . . . Fueron considerados textos de alcoba, eróticos, en alusión a Eros" (7). [And there's only mention of one volume of works. . . . They were considered texts of the bedroom, erotic, alluding to Eros.] Her tone is not antagonistic, but she is aware of the way *Canon de alcoba* has painted her image and left its mark upon the literary world. She introduces herself once again in *La letra de lo mínimo* by revisiting her childhood; recalling her family, her childhood friends, the anti-Semitic and racist sentiment common in Argentina of the era, the impact a book of photos with concentration camps had on her, and her impulse to write. She exhumes the politically oriented foundation of her upbringing, and in this spirit, the subsequent texts move further in the direction of the political.

Mercado's relationship with writing, whose therapeutic properties are evident in *En estado de memoria*, is evoked in the initial entries of *La letra de lo mínimo*. The act of writing her memories is a way for her to "conjure" the ghosts of the past:

En algún momento pude haber pensado que el relato que estaba escribiendo era una especie de *conjuro*, como si la evocación de algunas historias muy viejas, situadas en Córdoba, más concretamente entre los años cuarenta y cinco y cincuenta, disiparan, por la familiarización que operaba la escritura, los "fantasmas del pasado." (14)

At a certain point I may have thought that the story I was writing was some type of *exorcism*, as if by evoking some very old tales, that took place in Cordoba, between 1945 and 1950, the "ghosts of the past" would vanish under the spell of the written word.

She does indeed meditate on her early life in Córdoba, her family life, her first loves, and her marriage to her professor, Noé Jitrik. Córdoba and her childhood are the centerpieces of her autobiographical novel *La madriguera* (1996), which does not touch on the dictatorship period so much as it treats her family history and her formative years.

For Mercado, these "ghosts of the past" that she works to capture in *La letra de lo mínimo* are Chagallian figures floating just above the surface of the land, just above the surface of her consciousness. Her own experiences of exile, uprooting her from any firm connection with a particular place, impel her to reach for figures from her past and memorialize them, symbolically rooting them to the text, where they may come to life once again:

Bastó empezar a escribir para que lo que llamo mi caja, es decir mi casa o mi recinto separado del mundo que es la propia escritura (la de cualquiera), se poblara, en sucesivas acometidas nocturnas, durante el sueño y en el semi-sueño, de seres y objetos flotantemente chagallianos que parecían clamar por sus derechos: ellos estaban haciendo valer la pertinacia con que habían sobrevivido en mí y querían anclar en la tierra. Los traje, los até a la línea y ellos y sus circunstancias parecían contentarse con ese piso de realidad que es la página, o la pantalla—en el primer caso eran negro sobre blanco, en el otro tenían la suprema ocasión de ser trazos lumínicos en la oscuridad—. Pero no se quedaron allí. La acción cambiaba de sujeto: yo conjuraba, pero la escritura, por ese acto de "transmutación" de la materia, convocaba. (14)

Starting to write during successive nocturnal attempts, while asleep or half asleep, was enough to fill what I call my box, meaning my house or my own space apart from the world, which is one's writing (anyone's), with floating Chagallian beings and objects demanding their rights: they were asserting how long they had survived within me and wanted to take root in the soil. I carried them, I tied them to the line and they seemed to content themselves with the reality of the page, or the screen—in the first instance they were black on white, in the other they had the opportunity to become illuminated sketches in the darkness. But they didn't remain that way. The action changed subjects: I conjured, but writing, for its ability to "transform" material, summoned them to life.

Conjure implies something other than narration, or perhaps a specific mode of narration. *Conjure* implies a summons, sorcery, the practice of magic. *Conjure* implies a performance in that it works to restore an already performed behavior.[6] Mercado's memory work summons to life that which is otherwise forgotten and silenced. She proposes to have the ability to bring the remembered person or event to the "screen" in the sense that her written memories do not remain static but gain a dynamic presence. The reader, therefore, becomes spectator and witness to Mercado's memories. She restores images and people who she long thought disappeared from her life. For Mercado, writing is one of the most extreme forms of exercising consciousness: "La escritura es una de las formas más extremas de la conciencia porque es rastreo, desvelamiento, búsqueda de la imagen corroída y confusa que se despliega sobre un trasfondo y que sólo emerge cuando se la subleva, cuando se altera su estática" (19). [Writing is one of the most extreme forms of consciousness because it is the combing, relentless, search for the confusing and corroded image that unfolds over a background that only emerges when it is roused, when it's static condition is altered.] She begins deliberately practicing memory work to resuscitate the "perfiles y artistas que creía desaparecidos para siempre" (33). [profiles and artists that I thought had disappeared forever]. Consciously and emphatically, Mercado writes in order to combat melancholy:

> Y ése es mi modo de escribir *la memoria:* si digo *desenterrar,* estoy hablando de un acto que acaso permite sacar el objeto del olvido pero sin conferirle necesariamente vida: si digo *escarbar,* estoy buscando al azar un objeto perdido que se insinúa pero sólo se definirá en la medida de mi empeño por encontrolarlo, pero si digo *frotar* (en la lámpara de la memoria), ejecuto la voluntad de la invocación, digo tres deseos de rigor y ya estoy en la escritura, que sí, entonces, sería lo contrario de la melancolía. (34)

> And that is how I write *memory:* If I say *disinter,* I'm referring to an act that might allow me to prevent an object from being forgotten but without necessarily giving it life: if I say *rummage,* I'm casually looking for a lost object that's insinuated but only defined by my determination to find it, but if I say *rub* (the lamp of memory), I practice the desire to invoke, I make three rigorous wishes and I'm writing, which yes, then, would be the opposite of melancholy.

In a very literal manner, Mercado describes her writing as rescuing a memory from oblivion, keeping memory alive by inscribing it into the text, where it may continue evolving: "La tarea es poblar la línea, traer ese *adiós* a la página, reconocer en él un objeto perdido y hacerle un refugio, incluso inscribirlo en un paisaje que lo cobije y en el que la naturaleza juegue a voluntad sus evoluciones" (38). [The work is filling the line, bringing that *good-bye* to the page, recognizing the lost object in it and giving it refuge, even inscribing it into a landscape that shelters it and where nature allows it to evolve.]

Especially notable in *La letra de lo mínimo* are the texts "No me digas adiós" (Don't Say Goodye to Me), where she calls Manuel Puig back to life; "Napoleón Cardoza, el gato de Luis" (Napoleón Cardoza, Luis's Cat), where she recalls the Guatemalan writer Luis Cardoza y Aragón; and "Piedras de honda" (Rocks from the Deep), where Mercado brings to life a monument dedicated to victims of the Dirty War in Villa María, Córdoba. She recalls the deceased with such detail that the reader cannot help but visualize the poet Luis Cardoza y Aragón seductively brushing against a woman's thigh and reciting poetry to friends in his garden or Manuel Puig imitating Eartha Kitt singing "I wanna kiss, kiss, kiss, but you don't wanna."

In "Piedras de honda," Mercado animates the large, silent rocks that have been hauled from the sea to represent the seven Dirty War victims to whom they are dedicated. The author's act of remembering is not one of melancholy or nostalgia, but rather, an appeal to life, a resurrection:

> Por cierto, las pensé como memoria, pero nunca como lápidas ni como túmulos, nunca eternizadas por una decision sino eternas por la voluntad de los nombres que llevan, los siete nombres, que son los siete deseos vivos de ellos y de ellas: Ester Felipe, Luis Carlos Mónaco, Eduardo Requena, María Elena Viola, Aldo Apfelbaum, Elda María Francisetti, Eduardo Valverde. (70)

> Certainly, I thought of them as memory, but never as tombstones or tombs, never eternalized by choice but eternal due to the will of the names they carry, the seven names that are their seven living wishes: Ester Felipe, Luis Carlos Mónaco, Eduardo Requena, María Elena Viola, Aldo Apfelbaum, Elda María Francisetti, Eduardo Valverde.

As the reader can see in the image that opens this chapter, Mercado suggests that the reader, the spectator, the mourner internalize and taste these rocks in order to heighten awareness and spiritually awaken the memory of the seven victims: "Si se adentra en un ejercicio de reconocimiento y conciencia, estará con esos deseos y esos nombres" (70). [If one immerses themselves in an exercise of recognition and consciousness, s/he will be with those wishes and those names.] By naming the individuals who were murdered in the Dirty War, Mercado insists that the seven are no longer a statistic of victims, but individuals with passions, dreams, and families. Furthermore, by reinstating their individual identities, their names, she reverses the tyrannical dehumanization practiced by the dictatorial regime. Mercado's writing magnifies the images and people she describes. She weaves each memory so carefully that even Manuel Puig's five o'clock shadow becomes visible and admired by the reader.

The writing process practiced in *La letra de lo mínimo* is Mercado's struggle with melancholy. She has fought off the overwhelming displacement expressed in *En estado de memoria* and consciously works to disinter the dead by erecting spiritual tombs and restoring their identity. In this manner, the memories are not haunting. Rather, the dead are recognized as individuals and given refuge. Though one might argue that the establishment of monuments contributes to the archiving of history, and therefore to the silencing of the haunting memories of the disappeared, Mercado's text works to awaken the monument's vitality, showing that it is a performative space in which to practice the rituals of memory.

NARRAR DESPUÉS

Composed of six thematically arranged chapters, *Narrar después* is structurally more defined than the seemingly fragmented layout of Mercado's previous work. Her journalistic edge charges these brief thought-provoking entries—spanning the anthropological, sociological, and cultural—with an urgency that links them intimately to the moments in which they were written. Although somewhat similar, stylistically and thematically, to *La letra de lo mínimo*, *Narrar después* is considerably longer and even more politically oriented. Most importantly, *Narrar después* solidifies Mercado's commitment to Simón Dubnow's last words before being executed by the Gestapo in 1942: "*Shreibn un fashreibn!*" (Write and document history!) Indeed, "Un aire entra en el recinto cerrado" (Air Enters an Enclosure), where the Dubnow anecdote is found, lies at the heart of the collection, in the third chapter.

In the first two chapters, Mercado emphasizes her writing style; her relationship with *lo mínimo*, the often overlooked yet meaningful minutiae; and key historical events defining *después*, the aftermath, in which she writes—the Spanish civil war, World War II, the collapse of the Soviet Union, the fall of the Berlin Wall, the death of Ernesto Che Guevara, and the tragedy of Tlatelolco in Mexico—setting up a crescendo in the third chapter. In "Cementerio de papel" (Paper Cemetary), as implied in its title, Mercado's writing enters the throes of mourning.

In "Cementerio de papel," Mercado elaborates on some of her previous publications: the four texts nestled among the ripples of erotica spanning *Canon de alcoba;* the resonance of "La enfermedad" from *En estado de memoria;* and "Piedras de honda" (*La letra de lo mínimo*), the meditation on the monument to Dirty War victims of Villa María, Córdoba. Since the traditional cemetery fails to serve its purpose in the case of the tens of thousands of Argentine *desaparecidos* in a nation where the state has resisted (until very recently under Nestor Kirchner's presidency) initiating new trials against the generals and military officers acquitted during Carlos Menem's presidency and has resisted paying attention to the importance of memorials and commemorative ceremonies, the cemetery has become what Mercado calls a "paper cemetery": the disappeared are represented and mourned in newspapers, in published testimonies, and in posters carried around the Plaza de Mayo.[7] Boundless spaces of grief fill Argentina, where a counterculture, devoted to restoring to victims their identity and dignity, has been initiated by friends and family members of the *desaparecidos,* represented by such groups as the Madres de la Plaza de Mayo, the Abuelas, and H.I.J.O.S. Mercado, too, inscribes herself among this counterculture as she writes the names of disappeared individuals and carefully attends to the paper cemeteries circulating about her, attesting to the performative function of the texts she refers to in addition to her own writing.

In his work *The Untimely Present: Postdictatorial Latin American Fiction and the Task of Mourning* (1999), Idelbar Avelar astutely reads the subconscious of Mercado's work and analyzes her erection of exterior tombs in order to induce the labor of mourning, so essential to the healing of a wounded nation.[8] In *Narrar después,* Mercado's mourning work is a conscious effort. She emphatically notes in "Reapariciones" (Reappearances): "Reconstruyo los cuerpos" (111) [I reconstruct bodies]; "Yo, nosotros, nos tenemos que hacer cargo de los muertos (112). [I, we, have to take responsibility for the dead.] With the keen sense and determination of a skilled anthropologist coupled with the personal experience of living in the aftermath, Mercado studies the death notices, *tumbas de papel,* printed regularly in the Argentine newspaper *Página 12;* the stories sewn into the headscarves worn by the Madres de la Plaza de Mayo, *monumentos erigidos* (erected monuments), and carried as the Madres circle the Plaza, *cementerio en movimiento* (cemetery in motion) . It is in the individual stories narrated by the death notices, by photos, and sewn into kerchiefs, that breathe life into the disappeared: "La instancia personal y subjetiva rompe la desaparición, desarticula los designios que animaban sus ejecutores" (113). [The personal and subjective instance shatters the disappearance, foils the plans that enthused the executioners.] Otherwise, as asserted by Mercado, echoing Elie Wiesel's comments about the Holocaust, the executioner kills twice, the second time when he tries to erase the traces of the crime: "La palabra borrada y censurada, las imágenes tapadas, fueron una segunda muerte, una sobremuerte" (104). [The censored and erased word, the hidden images, were a second death, an overdeath.]

Whereas Avelar emphasizes the paradox that successful mourning work or restitution activates forgetting—it relegates the ghosts to the past by laying them to rest and suggests that Mercado is aware of this paradox while clinging to melancholy in *Estado de memoria*—it is evident in *La letra de lo mínimo* and *Narrar después* that Mercado believes the act of remembering the dead is a step toward achieving justice.[9] While working to restore to the victims the dignity denied them by their assassins, she climbs from melancholy into a "state of movement," *estado de movimiento*, where she recognizes that only recording this history and continuing to support entities such as Memoria Abierta, for which "Un aire entra en el recinto cerrado" was written, allow reconstruction of the lives of the Dirty War's disappeared victims.

In "Historias, memorias" (Stories, Memories), Mercado confesses that the experience of exile in Mexico has produced mutations, allowing her to see that the foreign is not necessarily "other." Whereas in "En que lugar" *(Canon de alcoba)*, she saw herself as a deformity, she realizes that her experience has forever changed her understanding of national identity and difference, aligning her with others who have experienced the margin, exile, and the trauma of grave losses:

> Aunque no se pueda ser mexicano, por razones obvias, haber vivido o vivir en México produce mutaciones, acaso ese híbrido nacional argentino-mexicano, el argenmex, designación que no parece tener su homología en Chile o Uruguay. . . . Creo que en cada uno gravitó lo mexicano y donde no se ha borrado ni atenuado el vínculo que nos unió a México esas marcas, o incitactiones, deberían estar: una manera de ver con una perspectiva de mayor ponderación lo propio y de menor distancia lo ajeno (133–34)

> Although one cannot be Mexican, for obvious reasons, having lived in or living in Mexico causes mutations, maybe that Argentine-Mexican national hybrid, the Argenmex, a designation that doesn't seem to have an equivalent in Chile or Uruguay . . ., I think Mexicanness gravitated to everyone and where that connection that united us with Mexico hasn't dissipated or

vanished, those marks, or developments, should exist: a perspective in which one ponders oneself more and others less.

Similar to the physically scarred boy of Gambaro's "Buscando la compañía del árbol," Mercado's condition of Argentine exile and "other" living in Mexico brings her close to Eva Alexandra Uchmany, a Holocaust survivor, who tells Mercado her childhood story of survival, one she would not disclose to others who had approached her previously. Mercado becomes the empathic listener for whom Uchmany was waiting for a long time, giving personal testament to the importance of empathic listeners in the aftermath of historical trauma, for the complex nature of narrating trauma leaves many stories untold. Undoubtedly, the unsettling experience of being Eva Alexandra's ideal listener has a powerful impact on Mercado:[10]

> La escritura, escribir, sería para mí eso: levantar el manto de las cosas, rescatarlas de su silencio y dejarlas decir. Esa larga tarde en la que Eva Alexandra me confió su relato comenzaba una nueva forma de ver y de hacer para mí de la que sólo ahora puedo darme cuenta: desprender del vasto mural de la historia con mayúsculas, que me apesadumbraba casi sin yo saberlo, una a una las láminas superpuestas y amalgamadas de esas historias personales que se me ofrecían para revelarme su sentido. Desprenderlas a medida que escribía en ellas y sobre ellas. (139)

> Writing, to write, for me is: uncovering things, rescuing them from silence and allowing them to speak. That long afternoon when Eva Alexandra confided her story to me, commenced a new way of seeing and doing things of which I'm only now able to comprehend: peeling off, one-by-one, the superimposed and amalgamated layers of those personal stories given me from the vast wall of history with capital letters, that had weighed upon me almost without my knowledge of it, in order to understand their meaning. Freeing them upon writing in and about them.

Mercado's meeting with Uchmany is followed by the aforementioned "Un aire entra en el recinto cerrado" where she evokes Dubnow's Yiddish exclamation before his death—*shreibn un fashreibn*—and makes the connection between the important role testimony has played in the aftermath of World War II, particularly for Holocaust survivors, and the need for it in the aftermath of Latin American dictatorships. Written for a presentation she gave at Memoria Abierta—the archival institution dedicated to collecting oral testimony of survivors and witnesses of the Dirty War, recognizing that the work done by the CONADEP was compromised by time limitations and institutional objectives—

Mercado praises the potential Memoria Abierta (Open Memory) offers to understanding history:

> Me detengo sobre el nombre acertado que designa el ámbito de este archivo oral: memoria abierta. La metáfora concentra una idea que subyace a toda búsqueda, a de abrir la memoria, la de abrir los archivos de una época o un tiempo, pero implica también un gesto de liberación, como si al abrir, un aire entrara en el recinto cerrado y actuara sobre las zonas necrosadas y yertas y las resignificara en una dimensión nueva. Lo que resurge, precisamente, es la dimensión soterrada de lo político y, de manera privilegiada, el modo en que esa acción política se inscribía en el día a día de protagonistas y testigos. Si algo rescata una historia de vida es la progresión de un deseo, el que latía en esas víctimas. (146)

> I meditate on the well chosen name that designates this oral history archive: open memory. The metaphor holds an idea that lies beneath all research, to open memory, to open the archives of an era or a time, but also implies a gesture of freedom, as if upon opening, air enters a cloister and passes over necrotic and stiff zones and redefines them in a new dimension. What resurfaces, exactly, are the buried politics, in a priviledged form, the way in which that political action inscribed itself in the day to day of the protagonists and witnesses. If anything is rescued by a life story it is the progression of a wish that lived inside those victims.

Evidently, Mercado is not only working through loss to mourn the individuals, but working toward social justice, to rescue the convictions and motivations driving those who were wrongfully murdered by the oppressive military forces of the dictatorial era. Furthermore, the connections Mercado makes between the aftermath of the Holocaust and Latin American dictatorships suggest that scholars of Latin American postdictatorship literature may find literary theories developed in the field of Holocaust studies particularly useful and appropriate.

In natural progression, chapter 3 is followed by a lighter movement. The reader is eased from the crypt in chapter 4, "Velada con señores" (An Evening with Men), where Mercado dedicates her writing to the patriarchal vestiges of soccer in Argentina and a series of vignettes ruminating on literature, art, and past loves. Her afternoon with Osvaldo Soriano, recalled in "Un destello amarillo" (A Yellow Flash), is especially moving. And "Otra vez Puig" (Puig Again) is a much appreciated sequel to "No me digas adiós" (*La letra de lo mínimo*), in which Mercado revisits Manuel Puig's novels and concludes: "El libro no cesa, siempre habrá otro que displace al anterior y que repita esa noción valorativa del antes y el después. Porque Manuel, en sus propios textos, logró la incesancia"

(195). [The book never ceases, because there's always another that displaces the one before and repeats the valuable notion of before and after. Because Manuel, in his own work, achieved endlessness.] Indeed, as the authorial role in Puig's novels betrays notions of a steady controlling authoritative voice commanding the text, his narrative opens up a polyphony of voices, silences, and positions for the characters and the reader alike.[11] As Mercado alludes to in *Narrar después*, the performance of storytelling throughout Puig's novels and the relationships the narrators form with their audience draw the reader to revisit and relive the worlds of Puig's work countless times. While the characters of *La traición de Rita Hayworth* (*Betrayed by Rita Hayworth*) "modeled their lives after the stars of the screen" (Levine 206), the transcendental nature of Molina's storytelling in *El beso de la mujer araña* (*Kiss of the Spiderwoman*) (1976) is example par excellence of the potential to *affect* the listener/reader/audience.[12] Though considerably different from Puig, in her vignettes Mercado affords her subjects a resounding presence that also transcends the text.

Chapter 5, "El no lugar" (The Non-Place), summons the experience of exile back to the surface in "Identidad" (Identity) and "La cápsula que soy" (The Capsule that I Am), but most notably, this chapter revisits the political. Especially powerful are her pieces that focus on the amnesty granted to military generals in the aftermath. In "Una pesadilla para Pinochet" (A Nightmare for Pinochet), where Mercado celebrates the much-awaited downfall of this bastion of fascism, she emphasizes that incriminating him works to heal the Chileans tortured by his regime: "Esa destrucción del General, a medida que prosigue indetenible, va reparando vastas zonas dañadas en la memoria de otros, sobrevivientes, víctimas" (207). [That destruction of the General, as long as he continues untouchable, repairs enormous wounded zones in the memory of others, survivors, victims.]

In a similar vein, "Los paseos del general" (The General's Walks), an elaboration of "Embajada" (Embassy) (*En estado de memoria*), reminds the reader that acquitted generals, guilty of masterminding the murder of thousands during the Dirty War, continue to walk the streets of impunity. As General Luciano Benjamín Menéndez walks freely through Córdoba, he reactivates the trauma of the Dirty War and symbolically erases the footsteps of his victims: "El general en las calles de Córdoba, pensé entonces, con su avance aparta y desplaza el andar de miles de personas que antes ocupaban el espacio de esa ciudad . . . y produce a su paso el trauma" (210–11). [The general in the streets of Córdoba, I thought, his gait separates and displaces thousands of people that previously occupied the city space . . . and he causes trauma along the way.] Memory and justice are intimately tied. Although Pinochet's health is finally failing and justice has begun to turn against him, Mercado reminds us that justice has yet to be served: "La verdad se conoce, la falta de justicia erosiona la dignidad, es una pesadilla de la historia de la que no podemos despertarnos todavía" (212). [The truth is known, the lack of justice erodes dignity, it's a historic nightmare from which we still cannot awaken.] Until the judicial system holds such generals accountable for their crimes, their continuous "innocent" presence in the public sphere reactivates the repressive nightmare of the Dirty War.[13]

The final chapter serves as a strong finale to *Narrar después*, complementing "Velada con señores" with meditations on the lives and memories of women in "Velada con señoras" (An Evening with Women): Mercado's own feminine genealogy dating from her great-grandmother to her daughter; Frida Kahlo's impact on an era; the shared experience of exile with the poet María Negroni; Doris Lessing's critique of feminism; Ramona, secret weaver and Comandante Zapatista; and praise of Margo Glantz's extensive literary and critical work. The final entry, written for a presentation of Glantz's novel *El rastro* (The Trace), serves as recapitulation; Mercado cites Avelar's definition of the literary crypt and suggests that the narrator of Glantz's work, Nora García, although dead, does not haunt the world she once occupied. Rather than wallow in melancholy, she exudes a dynamic vitality akin to the life I suggest Tununa Mercado's writing breathes into the aftermath. Mercado chooses to confront the phantoms and melancholic repercussions of the aftermath in *En estado de memoria*, reconciling with both her departure and her return. She wards off the return of melancholy through deliberate memory work practiced in *La letra de lo mínimo*. And in her most recent publication, *Narrar después*, Mercado pledges *shreibn un fashreibn*, to document history with an appeal to achieving justice in the aftermath.

15. "Parque de memoria." (Photo of the park devoted to the memory of the disappeared and victims of state terrorism in Ciudad Universitaria, Buenos Aires.) Photo by the author.

5

Staging the Crypt:
The Performance of Healing

IN HIS ARTICLE "POLÍTICAS DE MEMORIA Y DEL OLVIDO" (POLITICS of Memory and the Forgotten), Saúl Sosnowski questions the absence of monuments and spaces of commemoration dedicated to the *desaparecidos*, a phenomenon prevalent throughout the war-ravaged nations of Latin America:

> Why aren't there monuments to the disappeared in all of the countries affected by dictatorship? Is it due only to politics, accords between the victors, or because civil society—human rights movements aside—thinks in terms of the present and the short term future when monuments by definition are recuperations of the past and demand mourning and memory? One must demand the impossible: monuments and memorials in every detention center, in prisons, in concentration camps, and in the sunny everyday of neighborhoods, in the many different sites of repression. And even if designing monuments to the victims is achieved, will that be enough to complete the process of memory? Of course not, but it will be an inevitable step toward national restoration. (56)

One might argue that some of Sosnowki's demands have been met should one consider the 1999 inauguration of a park dedicated to the memory of the disappeared in Buenos Aires. However, this park is significantly isolated from the populace. Parque de la memoria is in Ciudad Universitaria, at least a one-hour bus ride from the urban center. In order to visit the park, one must take a deliberate journey to the recesses of memory, to the recesses of Buenos Aires.

I made this trip in July 2003 to find, much to my chagrin, that the park was still under construction and I was the sole visitor (see image at opening of this chapter). After roaming the park for some time, I finally came upon a trailer with a small sign stating "Comisión pro monumento a las víctimas del terrorismo de estado" (Pro-Monument

Commision for the Victims of State Terrorism). Once inside, I was given a brochure that explained the design of the park and the monuments that were already erected. The two principal monuments are, on the right, the cast iron arms reaching to the sky entitled *Victoria* (Victory), and on the left, the cubelike structure made of colored glass entitled *Monumento al escape* (Monument to the Escape). Both artists, William Tucker and Dennis Oppenheim, are North American. This visit posed many questions for me. What good is a park devoted to the memory of the disappeared if the park itself is in such a peripheral location, out of sight to all Argentines unless they make a lengthy trek to a rather desolate place? Is this the best that can be done to prioritize memory? Does the nationality of the artist hold importance when representing such nation-specific historical trauma? In that U.S. intervention supported the military operations during the Dirty War, how do Argentines feel about their tragedy being represented by U.S. artists? Is this just another attempt to appease the protesters and silence the population?

The conception of the park, its design and siting, took place during the ten-year presidency of Carlos Menem. For human rights activists and the sponsors of the Pro-Monument Commission, the establishment of this park dedicated explicitly to memory was considered a triumph. And rightly so, given that two significant incidents of terrorism took place in Buenos Aires during Menem's presidency—the bombing of the Israeli Embassy in 1992 and the bombing of the Jewish Cultural Center, the Asociación Mutual Israelita Argentina (AMIA), in 1994— both of which were largely unaddressed by the judicial system. It should also be noted that significant monuments devoted to the memory of the victims of these two bombings have been situated in peripheral locations: the Jewish cemetery, La Tablada, on the outskirts of greater Buenos Aires and a space under construction in the Parque de memoria. Further, since the rubble of the AMIA bombing was also dumped in the Ciudad Universitaria region, which hugs the Río de la Plata, where bodies of Dirty War victims have been discovered, more questions come to mind. How does this space differ from a cemetery?

Although one must remain critical when assessing efforts to commemorate the disappeared, because they are highly politicized, it is only very recently that Sosnowski's questions, and those of so many other Argentines, are seemingly being answered. March 24, 2004, the twenty-eighth anniversary of the *golpe*—the military coup that initiated the treacherous Dirty War of 1976–83—marked a significant change in the landscape of Argentine memory. Finally, the Argentine government is taking steps officially to remember and recognize the victims of the

Dirty War, the *desaparecidos*, estimated at 30,000. The Escuela Mecánica de la Armada (ESMA), where approximately 5,000 people had been tortured and killed, has officially been designated as a Museum of Memory. Although the structure of the museum is still being determined, portraits of General Jorge Rafael Videla and Admiral Emilio E. Massera, which once triumphantly adorned the walls of the ESMA, were officially removed by President Nestor Kirchner during the museum's inaugural ceremony.

Kirchner accompanied survivors into the ESMA to explore the cells where they had been held prisoners and tortured. For the first time, they entered without their blindfolds, and as heroes rather than subversives. As Pasquini Durán writes in "Justicia," the alliance of President Kirchner with monuments for human rights is one of the first "official" performances of reconciliation supported by the state:

> Finally, President Néstor Kirchner chose the legitimate and legal path, the only one compatible with the principles of democracy, to end the impunity and instill due and final justice. This year marks the first reconciliation between the force of the human rights movement and the actions of the State. Installing in the old center of the ESMA, bastion of clandestine extermination camps, a museum devoted to the memory of the victims of state terrorism is a symbolic act of reparation but, unlike his predecessors, Kirchner's raising the democratic bar and allowing plurality to breathe. Yesterday, in an initial act of emblematic possession, without mediative witnesses, the President, relatives of victims, and delegates of organizations visited what was once the terminal inferno for five thousand fellow countrymen.[1]

For survivors of the "terminal inferno," physically revisiting the crypt with acknowledgment and support from the state is the first step toward reconciliation with the past that has haunted them since the Dirty War. Such an act is a reversal of the "trastocamiento" staged in Gambaro's short story, for it welcomes the "unlistened-to" story into the "outside" world.

For Aldini, a survivor of the ESMA, returning is symbolic of an exorcism: "It was a test, crossing the space with a lot of internal ghosts. . . . Many said it was like an exorcism. It was being able to leave on our own accord and find people outside who were waiting for us. Back then, we occasionally entered and exited and the feeling that the outside was another world unaware of what happened on the inside was horrible."[2] For the first time, after having physically crossed the threshold that was denied him—he was blindfolded and "disappeared" while inside the ESMA—the world of the torture victim and that of the outside world are symbolically unified. Reclaiming the experience they were unable to externalize fully, because it had remained hidden and concealed, is crucial to undoing "entrapment." The act of finally usurping this haunted and haunting space from the military, so that Argentines may bear witness to the extermination center, one of hundreds throughout the nation, is an act that restores the victim's identity as a member of the polis. The survivor's experience is now officially acknowledged and shared with the community.

In her testimony, *A Single Numberless Death*, Nora Strejilevich concludes with a return to the Club atlético (Athletic Club), where she had been held prisoner and tortured. In her case, the physical detention center has been demolished and a road has been paved over it: "a road paved over our bodies suspended in a space that is no longer ours" (168). Although the physical edifice is no longer visible, Strejilevich insists on memory and retorts, "But names cannot be paved over . . . nor can souls. Names and souls have shapes that I can make out" (169). Her testimony—along with that of Alicia Partnoy, Alicia Kozameh, Jacobo Timerman, and others—is a monument or a "paper cemetery" where she unleashes "a chorus of voices resisting armed monologues that turned so much life into a single, numberless death" (171).

Are these acts—the establishment of the Museum of Memory and decrees to attend to justice and once again try the criminals guilty of involvement in the Dirty War—enough to heal the trauma the Dirty War has inflicted on the nation? They certainly work toward healing, on both the individual and collective levels, but of course, each individual experience of undoing "entrapment" is distinct and complex. By opening the dialogical principal regarding these dark years of Argentine history, such gestures do work toward achieving closure. As Sosnowski states, if monuments and public spaces of commemoration were to exist, "they would be an inevitable step toward national restoration."

Contemporary Argentine literature is both the product of trauma and a space to articulate trauma. Obliterating silence and revealing the torture that has pummeled the nation are essential in order for the nation to heal. As we have seen in stories like Bortnik's "Cuatro fotos" and ¿Te acordás?"; Gambaro's "El trastocamiento" and "Buscando la compañía del árbol"; and Mercado's "La enfermedad," narration is essential to lessening the pain of torture. These narratives speak to Elaine Scarry's assertion that all of "these other acts that restore the voice become not only a denunciation of the pain but almost a diminution of the pain, a partial reversal of the process of torture itself" (50). Such narratives cultivate a performative space for the release of the periperformative tension encompassing traumatic memory, so that it may find its voice.[3] These texts resist the cultural repression to forget the "unspeakable" or *lo innombrable* by producing narratives that expose the symptoms of traumatic victimization. By placing emphasis on this tense space, the threshold of the barely tolerable, and revealing the value of testimony and community, Bortnik, Gambaro, and Mercado encourage the act of narrating trauma, therefore cultivating potential empathy for the marginalized and victims of trauma, both as listeners within the text and as readers outside the text.

As Martha Nussbaum asserts in *Poetic Justice*, "Literary works typically invite their readers to put themselves in the place of people of many different kinds and to take on their experiences" (5). Thus, a literary work is capable of changing the reader, or at least the perspective of the reader. Given the silence that pervades society, when it comes to trauma, encouraging readers to open their hearts and minds to the realities of trauma survivors is an ethical task that these authors accomplish. As Susan Brison asserts, just as a being may be "undone" by violence, he or she may also be "remade in connection with others" (xi). Whereas the guest/survivor of Gambaro's "El trastocamiento," Cindal of Mercado's "La enfermedad," the protagonist of Bortnik's "El ultimo día," and the elderly couple of "Basta" are undone by society's refusal to acknowledge their experience and their pain, the woman who is shunned by her family in Gambaro's "Buscando la compañía del árbol," the protagonist of Bortnik's "¿Te acordás?" and Eva Alexandra Uchmany of Mercado's "Historias, memorias" are "remade" upon meeting kindred souls or empathic others and their pain grows lighter. The poor family and Sra. Schneider of Gambaro's "El misterio de dar" learn the importance of community in the act of telling/listening and the gesture of giving, while Ana of "El encuentro" is also permitted a space to remember her brother and construct a narrative that allows her to connect with the past, "no longer living" world.

These narratives unveil human misery, scars, and solitude so overlooked in a postdictatorship society encouraged to be indifferent in order to "look to the future." They do not turn the reader into "statues of salt" as Menem had promised but project a need for consciousness, solidarity, and compassion. By narrating trauma and memory, they facilitate a communicative act that helps "transform traumatic memories into narratives that can then be integrated into the survivor's sense of self and view of the world, but it also reintegrates the survivor into a sense of community" (Brison xi). Although this "integration into community" may not always be apparent within the narrative itself, readers or "secondary witnesses" of these stories may become *empathic listeners* and thus aid in fostering compassion and making space for trauma to be heard within society.

By exposing the "unlistened-to" story, their work gives individual voice to lift the blanket of historical trauma that has muffled Argentina's cry. Through the lens of trauma studies, their ethically charged works unveil the immense trauma that Argentine society has endured and must continue to work through, while also generating compassion. Furthermore, they not only give testimony to Argentina's national reality, but also expose repercussions that are symptomatic of the new global structure of relations and conflicts in other nations in contemporary society. Sixty years has passed since the end of the Holocaust and a new monument, designed by Peter Eisenman, has been inaugurated in Berlin in memory of the victims of Nazi extermination.[4] More than twenty years has passed since the end of Argentina's "Dirty War." Although the number of massacred was nowhere near that of the Holocaust, one might gather that the gesture of reclaiming the ESMA is only the beginning of a series of efforts to restore the shards of life abandoned in the Argentine concentration camps, filling the *boundless spaces of grief.*

My stay in Buenos Aires in July 2004 is a testament to this claim. Though only now climbing out of tremendous economic turmoil, Argentine theater and film are thriving. One need only glance over the *Espectaculos* section of *Página 12* or *La nación* to see that the performance of trauma is a physical reality in Buenos Aires, perhaps even a commodity. Films such as *Kamchatka*, narrated by a child whose parents were disappeared, and *Luna de Avellaneda*, emphasizing the fragmentation of Argentine society now immersed in corporate ventures, are extremely well attended, as well as stagings of Griselda Gambaro's *Decir sí* (Saying Yes) (1974), which was performed in the first cycle of Teatro Abierto; Eduardo Pavlovsky's *Telarañas* (Cobwebs) (1977); and Roberto Cossa's *La nona* (1977), all of which attend to the thin and sometimes permeable line separating victim from perpetrator and accomplice.

While I have moved away from theater in the discussion of the performance and performativity of trauma and narration, the prevalence of the dictatorship's repercussions on the screen and the stage today lends itself to further exploration of the ongoing performance of trauma in the aftermath. Especially notable is the formation of Teatro por la Identidad (Theater for Identity) *(TxI)*, a theatrical movement organized by the Abuelas de la Plaza de Mayo and *HIJOS*. Its express purpose is to incite its young audience to question their identity, with hopes of locating the over five hundred babies, now young adults in their twenties, who were born in the clandestine prisons of the Dirty War and given up for adoption.

Each cycle of TxI has shown approximately twenty short dramatic works. Although the first cycle solicited works from well-known Argentine dramatists, including Griselda Gambaro, the cycles now tend to solicit works from younger authors who have a more intimate connection with the generation the performances aim to affect. The 2004 cycle was held from June 28 to August 30 and featured twenty short plays performed every Monday night. Ten different theaters throughout Buenos Aires each hosted two plays. The turnout for all of the performances was immense. On my first attempt at seeing TxI, I waited on lines at three different theaters to no avail. The following week, I knew to arrive hours in advance and reserve a seat as soon as the theater opened. I attended *Hojas en blanco* (Blank pages) and *En lo de Chou* (At Chou's Place) at the Teatro Payró, the same theater where Pavlovsky's *Telarañas* was first performed in 1977.

Although my experience in the theater was much different from that of young Argentines who very well could be living a "changed identity," in the sense that they are unaware of their "true" identity, I could appreciate both the artistic and the activist nature of TxI. As TxI is described in its brochure: "It's a form of activism, of once again resuming theater's historical connection with reality. And it's a way of uniting actors, directors, writers, and the public in support of a noble goal, in a pursuit that finds us searching for our own identity." Undoubtedly, TxI merits interdisciplinary study. While the works of Teatro Abierto aimed to impact the consciousness of theatergoers who may unknowingly be accomplices to the dictatorial regime by giving in to the oppressive control administered by the military, TxI pressures young Argentines to question the homes they have been living in and the people they have considered family for the past twenty to thirty years. In terms of trauma studies, one would think that there would be great personal resistance to confronting such a loaded reality. And in terms of performance studies, assessing the impact of this theater would require not only an analysis of the works chosen for the stage and their production, but also a mode of inquiry spanning the sociological, psychological, and cultural to attend to the repercussions of these performances.

It is difficult to assess the way the performances affected the young spectators on the basis of my one experience in the audience, since I did not interview anyone or witness the repercussions the plays have had on their lives. According to the Abuelas, several of whom sat in the front row of the theater, a number of young men and women have gone to them and confessed that the performances have made them question their identities.

There is no doubt, however, that the encore performance, readings of passages from *Nunca más* by well-known Argentine actors, had a tremendous impact on everyone in the audience. As the well-known Argentine actor Daniel Fanego, stood in front of us insisting that he is lucky to know who he is—that his biological family is not a mystery—and then proceeded to read testimony aloud while photos of disappeared individuals were projected onto a screen, the climate of the theater was suddenly charged with the certainty of loss and the imperative to mourn the lives of particular individuals connected with the testimony and photos. The residue of the abstraction that hung in the air was instantly cleared and an exterior public tomb was erected for a collective mourning experience within the Teatro Payró.

Borrowing Walter Benjamin's reading of Klee's painting *Angelus Novus*, I suggest that the transformation of the crypt that is the ESMA into a space of memory is a symbolic act that allows the Angel of History—whose face is turned toward the wreckage of the past as a violent wind hurls him away—momentarily to close his wings and stay, to work to "awaken the dead, and make whole what has been smashed" (Benjamin 257). The "storm we call progress" has been momentarily calmed, letting up its resistance, so that the Angel can visit the destruction he has been pulled away from, therefore permitting him to "make whole what has been smashed" and work at potential healing.

Kirchner's government has empowered Argentina to look back at its past and enter the crypt both literally and metaphorically. *Cry for Me, Argentina*, as well, is an attempt to suspend the "storm" and visit the crypt so as to encounter the phantoms that haunt Argentina in the aftermath of the Dirty War, obviously still roaming Argentine stages, screens, and letters.

Notes

Chapter 1. Argentina in the Aftermath

1. Diana Taylor, "Trapped in Bad Scripts: The Mothers of the Plaza de Mayo," in *Disappearing Acts: Specters of Gender and Nationalism in Argentina's "Dirty War"* (Durham: Duke University Press, 1997), 183–222; "Performing Gender: Las Madres de la Plaza de Mayo," in *Negotiating Performance*, ed. Diana Taylor and Juan Villegas (Durham: Duke University Press, 1994), 275–305.

2. Marguerite Feitlowitz, *A Lexicon of Terror: Argentina and the Legacies of Torture* (New York: Oxford University Press, 1998), 13.

3. Ibid., 14.

4. David Rock, *Authoritarian Argentina* (Berkeley: University of California Press, 1993), 235.

5. Feitlowitz, *A Lexicon of Terror*, 111–12.

6. Unless otherwise noted, all translations are my own.

7. Gary Marx, "Argentina's President Pardons Leaders of 'Dirty War' on Leftists," *Chicago Tribune*, December 30, 1990.

8. Dori Laub, "Bearing Witness or the Vicissitudes of Listening," in *Testimony: Crises of Witnessing in Literature, Psychoanalysis, and History* (New York: Routledge, 1992), 69.

9. Jonathan Boyarin, "Space, Time, and the Politics of Memory," in *Remapping Memory: The Politics of TimeSpace*, ed. Jonathan Boyarin (Minneapolis: University of Minnesota Press, 1994), 23.

10. See Richard Schechner, *Performance Studies: An Introduction* (London: Routledge, 2002), 2.

11. Jorge Luis Borges, *Ficciones*, trans. and ed. Anthony Kerrigan (New York: Grove Press, 1962).

12. Kohut lists Antonio Di Benedetto, Humberto Constantini, Haroldo Conti, Marta Lynch, Rodolfo Walsh, Osvaldo Bayer, David Viñas, Marta Traba, Daniel Moyano, Griselda Gambaro, and Juan Gelman.

13. Enrique Medina, Juan José Saer, Luisa Valenzuela, Antonio Dal Masetto, Gerardo Mario Goloboff, and Abel Posse.

14. Ricardo Piglia, Vlady Kociancich, Osvaldo Soriano, Juan Carlos Martín, Jorge Asís, Mempo Giardinelli, César Aira, Reina Roffé, Miguel Bonasso, and Ricardo Monti.

15. Kart Kohut and Andrea Pagni, eds., *La literature argentina de hoy: De la dictadura a la democracia* (Frankfurt: Vervuert Verlag, 1989), 12.

16. Kohut mentions Saer, Piglia, Martini, Tomás Eloy Martínez, José Pablo Feinmann, Pablo Lerman, Rodrigo Fresán, Posse, Héctor Tizón, Martha Mercader, César

Aira, María Rosa Lojo, Lucio V. Mansilla, Giardinelli, Alicia Dujovne Ortíz, Osvaldo Soriano, Angélica Gorodischer, Noé Jitrik, Hebe Uhart, Ana María Shua, and Segio Chejfec.

17. Humor, spelled with the *r* inside the letter *o*, to allude to *humo* or smoke, hot air: a "progressive" Leftist biweekly magazine.

18. David William Foster, *Violence in Argentine Literature: Cultural Responses to Tyranny* (Columbia: University of Missouri Press, 1995), 188.

CHAPTER 2. "TALES FROM THE CRYPT"

1. All personal and anecdotal information about Aída Bortnik's life mentioned throughout this chapter has been attained during interviews I conducted with her during July 2004.

2. For a detailed account of the many levels and manifestations of censorhip during Argentina's Dirty War, see Andres Avellaneda, "The Process of Censorship and Censorship of the Proceso: Argentina 1976–1983," in *The Redemocratization of Argentine Culture, 1983 and Beyond*, ed. D. W. Foster (Tempe: Arizona University Press, 1989), 23–47.

3. *La historia oficial* was nominated for an Oscar for best screenplay and won first prize for original screenplay in the Festival de La Habana.

4. Foster, *Violence in Argentine Literature*, 62.

5. Avelar, *The Untimely Present*, 10.

6. In 1982, the principal illustrators and authors were Jorge Sabato, Tabaré, Mona Moncalvillo, Gloria Guerrero Ceo, Alfredo Grandona White, Hugo Paredero, Jorge Garayoa, and Carlos T. Braccamonte. Permanent contributors were Norberto Firpo, A. Vinelli, Walter Clos, Raúl Fortín, Tacha, Sanyú, Lawry, Suar, Meiji, Cilencio, Limura, Fontanarrosa, Marín, and Enrique Vázquez.

7. Annette H. Levine, "Entrevista con Andrés Cascioli," *Studies in Latin American Popular Culture* 25 (2006): 221–27.

8. John King, "Las revistas culturales de la dictadura a la democracia: El caso de *Punto de vista*," *Literatura argentina hoy*, ed. Karl Kohut and Andrea Pagni (Frankfurt: Vervuert Verlag, 1989), 87–94.

9. Roberto Bardini, "Entrevista con David Viñas," *HUM®* 119 (1983): 52–53.

10. *HUM®* 86, July 1982: 36–37.

11. Since all of Bortnik's stories excerpted in this chapter are only one page, I indicate only the page number for the first quotation from each story.

12. The photo that was used for her first stories was eventually replaced with a caricature of Bortnik done by Izquierdo Brown.

13. Rock, *Authoritarian Argentina*, 122.

14. Ibid., 138–39.

15. Wolfgang Iser, "The Reading Process: A Phenomenological Approach," in *Modern Criticism and Theory*, ed. David Lodge (London: Longman, 1988), 212–313.

16. Thomas Merton, ed., *Gandhi and Non-Violence* (New York: New Directions, 1965), 14.

17. Merton, *Gandhi and Non-Violence*, 11–12.

18. J. L. Austin, *How to Do Things with Words* (Cambridge: Harvard University Press, 1962), 6.

Chapter 3. "Empathic Unsettlement"

Griselda Gambaro, "Entrevista: Griselda Gambaro: La ética de la confrontación," in *Teatro*, ed. Miguel Angel Giella, Meter Roster, and Leandro Urbina (Ottawa: Girol, 1983), 31.

1. Premio Municipal, Ciudad de Buenos Aires; Premio Revista Talía y Seminario Teatral del Aire; Premio Argentores; Premio Nacional de Teatro; Premio de Investigadores y Críticos Teatrales; Premio de Fundación Di Tella.

2. Marcela Castro and Silvia Jurovietsky, "Decir no: Entrevista a Griselda Gambaro," *Feminaria literaria* 6, no. 11 (1996): 41–45.

3. Ibid., 43.

4. See the most notable works discussing Gambaro's novels: David William Foster's "Sexual Doing and Being Done," in *Violence in Argentine Literature: Cultural Responses to Tyranny* (Columbia: University of Missouri Press, 1995), 157–72; Susana Tarantuviez's *La narrativa de Griselda Gambaro: Una poética del desamparo* (Mendoza: Universidad Nacional de Cuyo, 2001); Silvia Murphy-Lorente's "La dictadura y la mujer: Opresión y deshumanización en *Ganarse la muerte* de Griselda Gambaro," in *La nueva mujer en la escritura de autoras hispánicas: Ensayos críticos*, ed. Juana A. Arancibia and Yolanda Rosas (Montevideo: Instituto Literario y Cultural Hispánico, 1995), 169–78; Hortensia R. Morell, "La narrativa de Griselda Gambaro: *Dios no nos quiere contentos*" *Revista Iberoamericana* 57, nos. 155–56 (1991): 481–94.

5. Diana Taylor, "Paradigmas de Crisis: La obra dramática de Griselda Gambaro," in *En busca de una imagen: Ensayos críticos sobre Griselda Gambaro y José Triana* (Ottawa: Girol, 1989), 11–23.

6. "Griselda Gambaro, "La difícil perfección," in *Griselda Gambaro, Teatro: Nada que ver: Sucede lo que pasa*, ed. Miguel Ángel Giella, Meter Roster, and Leandro Urbina (Ottawa: Girol, 1983), 31.

7. LaCapra, *Writing History, Writing Trauma*, 78.

8. During the first months of the dictatorship, in September 1976, seven adolescents from La Plata were kidnapped and tortured after demanding lower bus fares for students.

9. Elaine Scarry, *The Body in Pain* (New York: Oxford University Press, 1985), 3.

10. Julia Kristeva, *Powers of Horror: An Essay on Abjection* (New York: Columbia University Press, 1982), 4.

11. Nicolas Abraham, "Secrets and Posterity: The Theory of the Transgenerational Phantom," in *The Shell and the Kernel* (Chicago: University of Chicago Press, 1994), 166.

12. Sigmund Freud, "Mourning and Melancholia" in *General Psychology Theory* (New York: Collier, 1963).

13. LaCapra, *Writing History, Writing Trauma*, 70.

14. E. Husserl, *Experience and Judgment* (Evanston, IL: Northwestern University Press, 1973), 178.

Chapter 4. Paper Cemeteries

1. John Beverley, *Against Literature* (Minneapolis: University of Minnesota Press, 1993), 70–73.

2. All English excerpts from Tununa Mercado's *En estado de Memoria* are taken from Peter Kahn's translation.

3. See Rhonda Dahl Buchanan, "Eros and Writing in Tununa Mercado's *Canon de alcoba*," *Chasqui* 25, no. 1 (1996): 52–61; Myrna García-Calderón, "La escritura y el poder en *Canon de alcoba* de Tununa Mercado," *Revista Iberoamericana* 65, no. 187 (1999): 373–82; and Cynthia Tompkins, "La expansión del imaginario femenino: *Canon de alcoba* de Tununa Mercado," *Confluencia* 7, no. 2 (1992): 137–40.

4. See references to the survivor Mario Villani's testimony in chapter 3.

5. Sigmund Freud, *Moses and Monotheism*, trans. Katherine Jones (New York: Vintage Books, 1939), 84.

6. Richard Schechner, *Between Theatre and Anthropology* (Philadelphia: University of Pennsylvania Press, 1985), 36–37.

7. Jennifer Schirmer, "The Claiming of Space and the Body Politic within National Security States: The Plaza de Mayo Madres and the Greenham Common Women," in *Remapping Memory: The Politics of Time Space*, ed. Jonathan Boyarin (Minneapolis: University of Minnesota Press, 1994), 198.

8. Avelar, *The Untimely Present*, 9.

9. Ibid., 226.

10. Dori Laub, "Bearing Witness or the Vicissitudes of Listening," in *Testimony: Crises of Witnessing in Literature, Psychoanalysis, and History*,. ed. Shoshana Felman (New York: Routledge, 1992), 57–73.

11. Suzanne Jill Levine, *Manuel Puig and the Spider Woman* (Madison: University of Wisconsin Press, 2001), 206.

12. Ibid., 257–62.

13. Fernando Reati speaks to this issue in his introduction to *Memoria colectiva y políticas del olvido: Argentina y Uruguay, 1970–1990*, ed. Adriana J. Bergero and Fernando Reati (Rosario: Beatriz Viterbo, 1997), 17–18.

CHAPTER 5. STAGING THE CRYPT

1. J. M. Pasquín Durán, "Justicia," *Página 12*, March 20, 2004. http://www.pagina12.com.ar/diario/elpais/1-33040-2004-03-20.html

2. Victoria Ginzberg, "Qué importante sería que todos puedan ver esto: El presidente Kirchner recorrió la ESMA con sobrevivientes de esa cárcel clandestina," *Página 12*, March 20, 2004. http://www.pagina12.com/ar/diario/elpais/1-33037-2004-03-20.html

3. Eve Kosofsky Sedgwick, *Touching, Feeling. Affect, Pedagogy, Performativity* (Durham, NC: Duke University Press, 2003), 68.

4. Nicolai Ouroussoff, "A Forest of Pillars, Recalling the Unimaginable," *New York Times*, May 9, 2004, B1.

Bibliography

Abraham, Nicolas, and Maria Torok. *The Shell and the Kernel.* Chicago: University of Chicago Press, 1994.

Albuquerque, Severino J. *Violent Acts: A Study of Contemporary Latin American Theatre.* Detroit: Wayne State University Press, 1991.

Amante, Andrea. "De la casa a la plaza." *Feminaria literaria* no. 11 (1996): 46–48.

Améry, Jean. *At the Mind's Limits.* Translated by Sidney Rosenfeld and Stella P. Rosenfeld. Bloomington: Indiana University Press, 1980.

———. "Torture." In *Art from the Ashes: A Holocaust Anthology*, Edited by Lawrence Langer. New York: Oxford University Press, 1995.

André, Claudia. "En función de la palabra: Conversación con Tununa Mercado." *Alba de América* 16 (1998): 517–25.

Asis, Jorge. *Flores robadas en los jardines de Quilmes.* Buenos Aires: Losada, 1980.

Austin, J. L. *How to Do Things with* Words. Cambridge, MA: Harvard University Press, 1962.

Avelar, Idelbar. *The Untimely Present: Postdictatorial Latin American Fiction and the Task of Mourning.* Durham, NC: Duke University Press, 1999.

Avellaneda, Andrés. "Lecturas de la historia y lecturas de la literatura en la narrativa argentina de la década del ochenta." In *Memoria colectiva y políticas de olvido: Argentina y Uruguay, 1970–1990*, Edited by Adriana Bergero and Fernando Reati, 141–84. Rosario: Beatríz Viterbo, 1997.

———. "The Process of Censorship and Censorship of the Proceso: Argentina 1976–1983." In *The Redemocratization of Argentine Culture, 1983 and Beyond*, Edited by D. W. Foster, 23–47. Tempe: Arizona University Press, 1989.

Bakhtin, Mikhail M. *The Bakhtin Reader: Selected Writings of Bakhtin.* Edited by Pam Morris. London: E. Arnold, 1994.

———. *The Dialogic Imagination: Four Essays by M. M. Bakhtin.* Edited by Michael Holquist and translated by Caryl Emerson and M. Holquist. Austin: University of Texas Press, 1981.

Balderston, Daniel. *Ficción y política en la narrativa argentina.* Buenos Aires: Alianza, 1987.

Bardini, Roberto. "Entrevista con David Viñas." In *HUM®* 119 (1983): 52–53.

Benjamin, Walter. *Illuminations.* Edited by Hannah Arendt and translated by Harry Zohn. New York: Harcourt, 1968.

Bergero, Adriana, and Fernando Reati, eds. *Memoria colectiva y políticas de olvido: Argentina y Uruguay, 1970–1990.* Rosario: Beatríz Viterbo, 1997.

Bettelheim, Bruno. *The Informed Heart: On Retaining the Self in a Dehumanizing Society.* New York: Avon Books, 1971.

Beverley, John. *Against Testimony.* Minneapolis: University of Minnesota Press, 1993.

Bhabha, Homi. *The Location of Culture.* London: Routledge, 1994.

Bombal, María Luisa. "El árbol." In *Textos completos.* Santiago: Andrés Bello, 1983.

Borges, Jorge Luis. *Ficciones.* Madrid: Alianza, 1971.

———. *Ficciones.* Edited and translated by Anthony Kerrigan. New York: Grove Press, 1962.

Bortnik, Aída. "Ani-Nú y la belleza diferente." *HUM®* 61 (1981): 37.

———. "Basta." *HUM®* 87 (1982): 26.

———. "El baúl." *HUM®* 76 (1982): 46.

———. "Buscando." *HUM®* 81 (1982): 15.

———. "El corazón de Celeste." *HUM®* 84 (1982): 13.

———. "Crecé tranquilo." *HUM®* 70 (1983): 31.

———. "Cuatro fotos." *HUM®* 112 (1983): 11.

———. *De a uno.* Buenos Aires: Corregidor, 1983.

———. "Dieciocho años." *HUM®* 86 (1982): 11.

———. "Diferencia." *HUM®* 92 (1982): 17.

———. "Ella y los hombres." *HUM®* 60 (1981): 42.

———. "Ene la Perfecta." *HUM®* 65 (1981): 17.

———. "Hagamos una lista." *HUM®* 109 (1983): 20.

———. "Juguemos en el bosque." *HUM®* 63 (1981): 34.

———. "Julio montaña dorada." *HUM®* 111 (1983): 17.

———. "Mi tío Lito." *HUM®* 67 (1981): 19.

———. "Oferta." *HUM®* 89 (1982): 52.

———. *Papá querido: Teatro abierto: 21 estrenos argentinos.* Buenos Aires: Sociedad General de Autores de la república Argentina, 1981.

———. *Primaveras.* Buenos Aires: Teatro Municipal General San Martín, 1985.

———. "Socorro." *HUM®* 80 (1982): 13.

———. "¿Te acordás?" *HUM®* 73 (1981): 15.

———. "Tomás el ortodoxo" *HUM®* 62 (1981): 32.

———. "El último día" *HUM®* 69 (1982): 33.

———. "Un cuentito" *HUM®* 59 (1981): 31.

Boyarin, Jonathan. "Space, Time, and the Politics of Memory." In *Remapping Memory: The Politics of TimeSpace.* Edited by Jonathan Boyarin, 1–37. Minneapolis: University of Minnesota Press, 1994.

Brison, Susan J. *Aftermath.* Princeton, NJ: Princeton University Press, 2002.

Brooks, Peter. *Psychoanalysis and Storytelling.* Cambridge, MA: Blackwell, 1994.

Buchanan, Rhonda Dahl. "Eros and Writing in Tununa Mercado's *Canon de alcoba.*" *Chasqui: Revista de Literatura Latinoamericana* 25, no. 1 (1996): 52–61.

Caraballo, Liliana, Noemí Charlier, and Liliana Garulli. *La dictadura (1976–1983): Testimonios y documentos.* Buenos Aires: Ciclo Básico Común, 1996.

Carlson, Marvin. *Performance: A Critical Introduction.* New York: Routledge, 1996.

Caruth, Cathy, ed. *Trauma: Explorations in Memory.* Baltimore: Johns Hopkins University Press, 1995.

———. *Unclaimed Experience: Trauma, Narrative, and History.* Baltimore: Johns Hopkins University Press, 1996.

Castellanos, Rosario. *El eterno femenino.* México: Fondo de Cultura Económica, 1975.

Castillo, Debra. *Talking Back: Toward a Latin American Feminist Literary Criticism.* Ithaca, NY, and London: Cornell University Press, 1992.

Castro, Marcela. "Decir no: Entrevista a Griselda Gambaro." *Feminaria Literaria* 6, no. 11 (1996): 41–45.

Colás, Santiago. *Postmodernity in Latin America: The Argentine Paradigm.* Durham, N.C.: Duke University Press, 1994.

Colodro, Max. *El silencio en la palabra: Nombrar lo innombrable.* Providencia, Santiago, Chile: Cuarto Propio, 2000.

Cortés, Jason. "La teatralización de la violencia y la complicidad del espectáculo en *Información para extranjeros* de Griselda Gambaro." *Latin American Theatre Review* (2001): 47–61

Cossa, Roberto. "Gris de ausencia." In *Teatro Abierto 1981: 21 estrenos argentinos.* Buenos Aires: Corregidor, 1998.

———. "La nona." In *Roberto Cossa: Teatro 2.* Buenos Aires: de la Flor, 1989.

Dámaso Martínez, Carlos. "*En estado de memoria.* Tununa Mercado." *Babel* 18 (1990): 10.

DeHay, Ferry. "Narrating Memory." In *Memory, Narrative, and Identity.* Edited by Amritjit Singh, 26–44. Boston: Northeastern University Press, 1994.

Donghi, Tulio Halperín. "El presente transforma el pasado: El impacto del reciente terror en la imagen de la historia argentina." In *Ficción y política: La narrativa argentina durante el proceso militar.* Edited by Daniel Balderston, 71–95. Buenos Aires: Alianza Estudio, 1987.

Eagleton, Terry. "The Author as Producer." In *Marxism and Literary Criticism.* Berkeley: University of California Press, 1976.

Evangelista, Liria. *Voices of the Survivors: Testimony, Mourning, and Memory in Post-Dictatorship Argentina (1983–1995).* Translated by Renzo Llorente. New York: Garland, 1998.

Falicov, Tamara L. "Film Production in Argentina under Democracy: 1983–1989: The Official Story (La Historia oficial) as an International Mind." *The Southern Quarterly* 39, no. 4 (2001): 123–34.

Feitlowitz, Marguerite. "Argentina: aquí la vida es normal." In *El viejo topo* 77 (n.d.): 36–55.

———. "Crisis, Terror, and Disappearance: The Theatre of Griselda Gambaro." In *Theatre* 21 (1990): 34–38.

———. *A Lexicon of Terror: Argentina and the Legacies of Torture.* New York: Oxford University Press, 1998.

Felman, Shoshana, and Dori Laub, eds. *Testimony: Crises of Witnessing in Literature, Psychoanalysis, and History.* New York: Routledge, 1992.

Foster, David William. "Los parámetros de la narrative argentina durante el 'proceso de reorganización nacional." In *Ficción y política: La narrativa argentina durante el pro-*

ceso militar. Edited by Daniel Balderston, 96–108. Buenos Aires: Alianza Estudio, 1987.

———. *Violence in Argentine Literature: Cultural Responses to Tyranny.* Columbia: University of Missouri Press, 1995.

Foucault, Michel. "Space, Knowledge, and Power." In *The Foucault Reader.* Edited by Paul Rabinow, 239–56. New York: Panteón, 1984.

———. "Truth and Power." In *The Foucault Reader.* Edited by Paul Rabinow, 51–75. New York: Panteón, 1984.

Franco, Jean. *The Decline and Fall of the Lettered City.* Cambridge, MA: Harvard University Press, 2002.

———. "Invadir el espacio público: transformar el espacio privado" *Debate Feminista* 8 (1993): 267–87.

Fraser, Nancy. "Rethinking the Public Sphere: A Contribution to the Critique of Actually Existing Democracy." In *Habermas and the Public Sphere.* Edited by Ed Craig, 109–42. Cambridge, MA: MIT Press, 1992.

Fresco, Nadine. "Remembering the Unknown." In *International Review of Psychoanalysis* 11 (1984): 417–27.

Freud, Sigmund. *Moses and Monotheism.* Translated by Katherine Jones. New York: Vintage, 1939.

———. "Mourning and Melancholia." In *General Psychological Theory.* Edited by Philip Rieff, 164–79. New York: Collier Books, 1963.

Friedlander, Saul. "Trauma, Memory, and Transference." In *Holocaust Remembrance, the Shapes of Memory.* Edited by Geoffrey Hartman. Cambridge: Blackwell, 1994.

Gambaro, Griselda. *Antígona furiosa.* Buenos Aires: Ediciones de la Flor, 1988.

———. *Atando cabos.* Buenos Aires: Ediciones de la Flor, 1996.

———. *El campo.* Buenos Aires: Ediciones Insurexit, 1968.

———. *La casa sin sosiego.* Buenos Aires: Ricordi Americana, 1992.

———. *Del sol naciente.* Buenos Aires: Ediciones de la Flor, 1989.

———. *El desatino.* Buenos Aires: Emece Editoriales, 1965.

———. *Dios no nos quiere contentos.* Buenos Aires: 1979.

———. *Información para extranjeros.* Buenos Aires: Ediciones de la Flor, 1987.

———. *La malasangre.* Buenos Aires: Ediciones de la Flor, 1989.

———. *Lo mejor que se tiene.* Buenos Aires: Norma, 1998.

———. *Las paredes.* Barcelona: D.L. 1966.

———. "Los rostros del exilio." *Alba de América: Revista Literaria* 7, nos. 12–13 (1989): 31–35.

———. *Los siameses.* Buenos Aires: Ediciones Insurexit, 1967.

García-Calderón, Myrna. "La escritura erótica y el poder en *Canon de alcoba* de Tununa Mercado." *Revista Iberoamericana* 65, no. 187 (1999): 373–82.

Garfield, Evelyn Picon. *Women's Voices from Latin America: Interviews with Six Contemporary Authors.* Detroit: Wayne State University Press, 1985.

Gelder, Ken. *Reading the Vampire.* New York: Routledge, 1994.

Genette, Gerard. *Paratexts: Thresholds of Interpretation.* New York: Cambridge University Press, 1997.

Giella, Miguel Angel, Peter Roster, and Leandro Urbina, eds. *Griselda Gambaro. Teatro: Nada que ver, Sucede lo que pasa.* Ottawa: Girol, 1983.

Ginzberg, Victoria. "Qué importante sería que todos puedan ver esto: El presidente Kirchner recorrió la ESMA con sobrevivientes de esa cárcel clandestina." *Página12* (March 20, 2004). http://www.pagina12.com.ar/diario/elpais/1-33037-2004-03-20.html (acceessed March 20, 2004).

Glantz, Margo. "*En estado de memoria.*" *La Jornada Semanal* 163 (1992): 43–46.

Gogol, Nikolai. "The Overcoat." In *Diary of a Madman and Other Stories.* New York: New American Library, 1960.

Gorostiza, Carlos. "El acompañamiento." In *Teatro Abierto 1981: 21 estrenos argentinos.* Buenos Aires: Corregidor, 1998.

Graham-Jones, Jean. "Decir 'No': El aporte de Bortnik, Gambaro y Raznovich al Teatro Abierto '81." In *Teatro argentino durante El Proceso (1976–1983).* Edited by Juana Arancibia and Zulema Mirkin, 181–97. Buenos Aires: Vinciguerra, 1992.

Guy, Donna J. *Sex and Danger in Buenos Aires: Prostitution, Family, and Nation in Argentina.* Lincoln: University of Nebraska Press, 1991.

Haight, Barbara K. *The Art and Science of Reminiscing: Theory, Research, Methods, and Applications.* Vancouver: Taylor and Francis, 1991.

Halbwachs, Maurice. *On Collective Memory.* Edited and translated by Lewis A. Coser. Chicago: University of Chicago Press, 1992.

Held, Virginia. *Feminist Morality: Transforming Culture, Society, and Politics.* Chicago: University of Chicago Press, 1993.

Herman, Judith L. *Trauma and Recovery: The Aftermath of Violence, from Domestic Abuse to Political Terror.* New York: Basic Books, 1992.

Hernández-Araico, Susana. "Cinematografía excepcional: Arte, popularidad y protesta de una guionista argentina." *Alba de América: Revista literaria* 5, nos. 8–9 (1987): 363–70.

Hirsch, Marianne. *Family Frames: Photography, Narrative and Postmemory.* Cambridge, MA: Harvard University Press, 1997.

———. "Surviving Images: Holocaust Photography and the Work of Postmemory." *The Yale Journal of Criticism* 14, no. 1 (2001): 5–37.

Husserl, E. *Experience and Judgment.* Translated by J. S. Churchill and K. Ameriks. Evanston: Northwestern University Press, 1973.

Hutcheon, Linda. "The Pastime of Past Time." In *Essentials of the Theory of Fiction.* Edited by Michael J. Hoffman and Patrick D. Murphy, 473–95. Durham: Duke University Press, 1996.

———. *A Poetics of Postmodernism.* New York: Routledge, 1988.

———. *The Politics of Postmodernism.* London: Routledge, 1989.

———. *A Theory of Parody: The Teachings of Twentieth-Century Art Forms.* New York: Methuen, 1985.

Huyssen, Andreas. *Twilight Memories: Marking Time in a Culture of Amnesia.* New York: Routledge, 1995.

Ingarden, Roman. *The Literary Work of Art.* Translated by Ruth Ann Crowley and Kenneth R. Olson. Evanston, IL: Northwestern University Press, 1973.

Iser, Wolfgang. "The Reading Process: A Phenomenological Approach." In *Modern Criticism and Theory*. Edited by David Lodge, 212–28. London: Longman, 1988.

Jaquette, Jane S. ed. *The Women's Movement in Latin America: Feminism and the Transition to Democracy*. Boston: Unwin Hyman, 1989.

Jehenson, Myriam Yvonne. "Staging Cultural Violence: Griselda Gambaro and Argentina's 'Dirty War.' " *Mosaic: A Journal for the Interdisciplinary Study of Literature* 32, no. 1 (1999): 85–104.

Kaminsky, Amy K. *After Exile: Writing the Latin American Diaspora*. Minneapolis: University of Minnesota Press, 1999.

———. *Reading the Body Politic: Feminist Criticism and Latin American Women Writers*. Minneapolis: University of Minnesota Press, 1993.

Kohut, Karl, and Andrea Pagni, eds. *Literatura Argentina hoy: de la dictadura a la democracia*. Frankfurt: Vervuert, 1989.

Kozameh, Alicia. *Pasos bajo el agua*. Buenos Aires: Contrapunto, 1987.

King, John. "Las revistas culturales de la dictadura a la democracia: el caso *Punto de Vista*." In *Literatura argentina hoy*. Edited by K. Kohut and A. Pagni. Frankfurt: Verveurt Verlag, 1989.

Kristeva, Julia. *Black Sun: Depression and Melancholia*. New York: Columbia University Press, 1984.

———. *Powers of Horror: An Essay on Abjection*. New York: Columbia University Press, 1982.

Kundera, Milan. *The Book of Laughter and Forgetting*. London: Faber & Faber, 1982.

Lacan, Jaques. *Four Fundamental Concepts of Psycho-Analysis*. New York: Norton, 1981.

LaCapra, Dominick. *History and Memory after Auschwitz*. Ithaca, NY: Cornell University Press, 1998.

———. *Representing the Holocaust: History, Theory, and Trauma*. Ithaca, NY: Cornell University Press, 1994.

———. *Writing History, Writing Trauma*. Baltimore: Johns Hopkins University Press, 2001.

Langer, Lawrence. *Holocaust Testimonies, the Ruins of Memory*. New Haven, CT: Yale University Press, 1991.

Laub, Dori. "Bearing Witness or the Vicissitudes of Listening." In *Testimony: Crises of Witnessing in Literature, Psychoanalysis, and History*. Edited by Dori Laub and Shoshana Felman, 57–73. New York: Routledge, 1992.

———. "Truth and Testimony: The Process and the Struggle." In *Trauma: Explorations in Memory*. Edited by Cathy Caruth, 61–75. Baltimore: Johns Hopkins University Press, 1995.

Levi, Primo. *The Drowned and the Saved*. Translated by Raymond Rosenthal. New York: Summit Books, 1988.

———. *If Not Now, When?* New York: Penguin. 1985.

———. *Survival in Auschwitz*. Translated by Stuart Woolf. New York: Touchstone. 1996.

Levine, Annette H. "Entrevista con Andrés Cascioli: La revista *HUM®* y la Guerra Sucia." *Studies in Latin American Popular Culture* 25 (2006): 221–27.

Levine, Suzanne Jill. *Manuel Puig and the Spider Woman.* Madison: University of Wisconsin Press, 2001.

Logan, Joy. "A Study on Exile and Subjectivity: Locating the Self in Tununa Mercado's *En estado de memoria.*" *Revista Hispanica Moderna* 50, no. 2 (1997): 391–402.

López Oncón, M. "La literatura del silencio. Reportaje a tres narradores argentinos." *La opinión cultural* (1981): iv.

Lorente-Murphy, Silvia. "La dictadura y la mujer: Opresión y deshumanización en Ganarse la muerte de Griselda Gambaro." In *La nueva mujer en la escritura de autoras hispanicas: Ensayos críticos.* Edited by Juana Arancibia and Yolanda Rosas, 169–78. Montevideo: Instituto Literario y Cultural Hispanico, 1995.

Maree, Cathy. "Theatre and the Struggle of Memory against Forgetting in Spain, Latin America and South Africa." *Journal of Literary Studies* 14, nos. 3–4 (1998): 299–321.

Maristany, José Javier. *Narraciones peligrosas: Resistencia y adhesión en las novelas del Proceso.* Buenos Aires: Biblos, 1999.

Martínez, Tomás Eloy "La Argentina de Borges y Perón." *HUM®* 269 (1990): 32–38.

Masiello, Francine. "La argentina durante el Proceso: las múltiples resistencias de la cultura." In *Ficción y Política: La narrative argentina durante el proceso militar.* Edited by Daniel Balderston, 11–29. Buenos Aires and Madrid: Alianza, 1987.

———. *The Art of Transition: Latin American Culture and Neoliberal Crisis.* Durham, NC: Duke University Press, 2001.

Mazziotti, Nora. "Lo cotidiano enrarecido: *De a uno,* de Aída Bortnik." In *Teatro argentino durante el proceso (1976–1983).* Edited by Juana Arancibia and Zulema Mirkin, 91–97. Buenos Aires: Vinciguerra, 1992.

———. *Poder, deseo y marginación: Aproximaciones a la obra de Griselda Gambaro.* Buenos Aires: Puntosur, 1989.

Mercado, Tununa. *Canon de alcoba,* Buenos Aires: A. Korn, 1988.

———. *Celebrar a la mujer como a una pascua.* Buenos Aires: Jorge Alvarez, 1967.

———. *En estado de memoria.* Córdoba: Alción, 1998.

———. *La letra de lo mínimo.* Rosario: B. Viterbo Editora, 1994.

———. *La madriguera.* Buenos Aires: Tusquets Editores, 1996.

———. *Narrar después.* Rosario: B. Viterbo, 2003.

Merton, Thomas, ed. *Gandhi and Non-Violence.* New York: New Directions, 1965.

Meson, Danusia L. "The Official Story: An Interview with Aída Bortnik." *Cineaste* 14, no. 4 (1986): 30–35.

Mizraje, María Gabriel. "Morder la tradición: El *Nosferatu* de Griselda Gambaro." In *Latin American Theatre Review* (2002): 79–84.

Molloy, Silvia. *At Face Value: Autobiographical Writing in Spanish America.* Cambridge: Cambridge University Press, 1991.

Mora, Gabriela. "Tununa Mercado." *Hispamerica: Revista de Literatura* 21, no. 62 (1992): 137–40.

———. "Tununa Mercado." In *Revista de Crítica Literaria Latinoamericana* 31 (1990): 77–81.

Moreiras, Alberto. "The Aura of Testimonio." In *The "Real" Thing: Testimonial Discourse in Latin America.* Edited by George M. Gugelberger. Durham, NC: Duke University Press, 1996.

———. "Pastiche Identity and Allegory of Allegory." In *Latin American Identity and Constructions of Difference.* Edited by Amaryll Chanady, 204–37. Minneapolis and London: Minessota University Press, 1994.

———. "Postdictadura y reforma del pensamiento." *Revista de Crítica Cultural* 7 (1993): 26–35.

Morell, Hortensia R. "La narrativa de Griselda Gambaro: *Dios no nos quiere contentos.*" *Revista Iberoamericana* 57, nos. 155–56 (1991): 481–94.

Moyano, Daniel. *El vuelo del tigre.* Madrid: Legasa, 1981.

Munoz, Eugenia. "El silencio y la ruptura con el orden patriarcal en La malasangre de Griselda Gambaro." In *Selected Proceedings: Louisiana Conference on Hispanic Languages and Literatures.* Edited by Joseph V. Ricapito, 169–78. Baton Rouge: Louisiana State University Press, 1994.

Nussbaum, Martha. *Poetic Justice.* Boston: Beacon, 1995.

O'Connell, Patrick L. "Individual and Collective Identity through Memory in Three Novels of Argentina's 'El proceso.'" In *Hispania* 81, no. 1 (1998): 31–41.

———. "Homecoming and Identity in the Autobiographical Narrative of Tununa Mercado." *Chasqui-Revista de Literatura Latinoamericana.* 27, no. 2 (1998): 106–15.

Ostrov, Andrea. "*Canon de alcoba:* una pornografía de la diferencia." *Hispamerica: Revista de Literatura* 22, no. 66 (1993): 99–108.

Ourousoff, Nicolai. "A Forest of Pillars, Recalling the Unimaginable." In *New York Times,* May 9, 2004, B1.

Partnoy, Alicia. *The Little School: Tales of Disappearance and* Survival. San Francisco: Cleiss Press, 1998.

Pasquini Durán. "Justicia." *Página 12,* March 20, 2004. http://www.pagina12.com.ar/diario/elpais/1-33040-2004-03-20.html (accessed March 20, 2004).

Pavel, Thomas. *Fictional Worlds.* Cambridge, MA: Harvard University Press, 1986.

Pavlovsky, Eduardo. *Telarañas.* In *Teatro Completo II.* Buenos Aires: Atuel, 1998.

Perelli, Carina. "Memoria de Sangre: Fear, Hope and Disenchantment in Argentina." In *Remapping Memory: The Politics of TimeSpace.* Edited by Jonathan Boyarin, 39–66. Minneapolis: University of Minnesota Press, 1994.

Peterka, Martha Lane. *The Argentine Novel in the 1970s: The Generation of '76.* PhD Diss., University of Missouri-Columbia, 1988.

Pfeifer, Erna. *Exiliadas, emigrantes, viajeras: Encuentro con diez escritoras latinoamericanas.* Frankfurt: Verveurt Iberoamericana, 1995.

Piglia, Ricardo. *Crítica y ficción.* Buenos Aires: Siglo Veinte, 1990.

———. *Respiración artificial.* Buenos Aires: Editorial Pomaire, 1980.

Plaza, Ramón. "Tununa Mercado: *En estado de memoria.*" *Utopías del Sur* 5 (1990): 3–6.

Pratt, Mary Louise. "Criticism in the Contact Zone: Decentering Community and Nation." In *Critical Theory, Cultural Politics, and Latin American Narrative.* Edited by Steven Bell, Albert LeMay, and Leonard Orr, 83–102. Notre Dame, IN: University of Notre Dame Press, 1993.

———. *Toward a Speech Act Theory of Literary Discourse*. Bloomington: Indiana University Press, 1977.

———. "Women, Literature, and National Brotherhood." *Nineteenth Century Contexts* 18, no. 1 (1994): 27–47.

Puig, Manuel. *El beso de la mujer araña*. Barcelona: Seix Barral, 1976.

———. *La traición de Rita Hayworth*. Buenos Aires: Jorge Alvarez, 1968.

Ramsey, Cynthia. "The Official Story: Feminist Re-Visioning as Spectator Response." *Studies in Latin American Popular Culture* 11 (1992): 157–69.

Reati, Fernando Oscar. *Nombrar lo innombrable: Violencia política y novela argentina, 1975–85*. Buenos Aires: Legasa, 1992.

Richard, Nelly "Bordes, diseminación, postmodernismo: una metáfora latinoamericana de fin de siglo." In *Las culturas de fin de siglo en América Latina*. Edited by Josefina Ludmer, 240–48. Buenos Aires: Beatriz Viterbo, 1994.

———. *Residuos y metáforas: Ensayos de crítica cultural sobre el Chile de la Transición*. Santiago: Cuarto propio, 1998.

Rickels, Lawrence A. *Aberrations of Mourning: Writing on German Crypts*. Detroit: Wayne State University Press, 1988.

———. *The Vampire Lectures*. Minneapolis: University of Minnesota Press, 1999.

Rock, David. *Authoritarian Argentina: The Nationalist Movement, Its History and Its Impact*. Berkeley: University of California Press, 1993.

Roffé, Reina. *Conversaciones americanas de la escritora y periodista argentina Reina Roffé*. Madrid: Páginas de Espumas, 2001.

———. "Entrevista a Griselda Gambaro." *Cuadernos Hispanoamericanos* 588 (1999): 111–24.

Saavedra, Guillermo. "El arte de recordar la propia letra." In *La curiosidad impertinente: Entrevistas con narradores argentinos*. Edited by Guillermo Saavedra, 31–42. Rosario: Beatriz Vitebro, 1993.

Saer, Juan José. *Nadie, nada, nunca*. México: Siglo XXI, 1980.

Sarlo, Beatriz. "El campo intelectual: Un espacio doblemente fracturado." In *Represión y reconstrucción de una cultura: El caso argentino*. Edited by Saúl Sosnowski, 95–107. Buenos Aires: Editorial Universitaria, 1988.

———. *Escenas de la vida postmoderna: Intelectuales, arte y videocultura en la Argentina*. Buenos Aires: Ariel, 1994.

———. "No olvidar la Guerra de Malvinas: sobre cine, literatura e historia." In *Punto de vista* 49 (1994): 11–14.

Scarry, Elaine. *The Body in Pain: The Making and Unmaking of the World*. New York: Oxford University Press, 1985.

Schechner, Richard. *Between Theater and Anthropology*. Philadelphia: University of Pennsylvania Press, 1985

———. *Performance Studies: An Introduction*. London: Routledge, 2002

Schirmer, Jennifer. "The Claiming of Space and the Body Politic within National Security States: The Plaza de Mayo Madres and the Greenham Common omen." In *Remapping Memory: The Politics of Time Space*. Edited by Jonathan Boyarin, 185–220. Minneapolis: University of Minnesota Press, 1994.

Schnaith, Nelly. "Imaginar: ¿Juego o compromiso?: Conversación con Griselda Gambaro." *Quimera: Revista de Literatura* 24 (1982): 47–50.

Sedgwick, Eve Kosovsky. *Touching Feeling: Affect, Pedagogy, Performativity.* Durham, NC: Duke University Press, 2003.

Shay, Jonathan. *Achilles in Vietnam: Combat Trauma and the Undoing of Character.* New York: Atheneum, 1994.

Shua, Ana María. *Soy paciente.* Buenos Aires: Losada, 1980.

Silverman, Kaja. *World Spectators.* Stanford, CA: Stanford University Press, 2000.

Singh, Amritjit. *Memory, Narrative, and Identity.* Boston: Northeastern University Press, 1994.

Somigliana, Carlos. "El nuevo mundo." In *Teatro Abierto 1981: 21 estrenos argentinos.* Buenos Aires: Corregidor, 1998.

Sontag, Susan. *On Photography.* New York: Farrar, 1973.

Soriano, Osvaldo. *No habrá más penas ni olvido.* Barcelona: Bruguera, 1980.

———. *Una sombra ya pronto serás.* Madrid: Mondadori España, 1991.

Sosnowski, Saúl, ed. *Represión y reconstrucción de una cultura: El caso argentino.* Buenos Aires: Editorial universitaria, 1988.

———. "Políticas de la memoria y del olvido." In *Memoria colectiva y políticas de olvido: Argentina y Uruguay, 1970–1990.* Edited by Adriana Bergero and Fernando Reati, 43–58. Rosario: Beatriz Viterbo, 1997.

Spiller, Roland. *La novela argentina de los años 80.* Frankfurt: Vervuert Verlag, 1991.

Strejilevich, Nora. *A Single Numberless Death.* Translated by Cristina de la Torre. Charlottesville: University of Virginia Press, 2002.

Summers, Hollis, ed. *Discussions of the Short Story.* Boston: D. C. Heath, 1963.

Tarantuviez, Susana. *La narrativa de Griselda Gambaro: Una poética del desamparo.* Mendoza: Universidad Nacional de Cuyo, 2001.

Taylor, Diana. *The Archive and the Repertoire: Performing Cultural Memory in the Americas.* Durham, NC: Duke University Press, 2003.

———. *Disappearing Acts: Spectacles of Gender and Nationalism in Argentina's "Dirty War."* Durham, NC: Duke University Press, 1997.

———. "Performing Gender: Las Madres de la Plaza de Mayo." *Negotiating Performance.* Edited by Diana Taylor and Juan Villegas, 275–305. Durham, NC: Duke University Press, 1994.

———. *Theatre in Crisis: Drama and Politics in Latin America.* Lexington: Kentucky University Press, 1992

Terdiman, Richard. *Present Past: Modernity and the Memory Crisis.* Ithaca, NY: Cornell University Press, 1993.

Teski, Marea, and Jacob J. Climo. *The Labyrinth of Memory.* Westport, CT: Bergin & Garvey, 1995.

Tierney-Tello, Mary Beth. *Allegories of Transgression and Transformation: Experimental Fiction by Women under Dictatorship.* Albany, NY: SUNY Press, 1996.

Timerman, Jacobo. *Prisoner without a Name, Cell without a Number.* New York: Knopf, 1981.

Tissera, Ana. "Tununa Mercado: La memoria del sur en *En estado de memoria.*" In *De centros y periferias en la literatura de Córdoba.* Edited by Mirian Pino and Fernando Reati, 25–40. Córdoba: Ruben, 2001.

Tompkins, Cynthia. "La palabra, el deseo, el cuerpo o la expansión del imaginario femenino: *Canon de alcoba* de Tununa Mercado." *Confluencia: Revista Hispanica de Cultura y Literatura.* 7, no. 2 (1992): 137–40.

Uribe, Ogla T. "Modelos narrativos de homosexualidad y heterosexualidad en el reino de los sentidos de *Canon de alcoba.* "Ver," "Oír" y "El recogimiento": tres textos de Tununa Mercado." *Latin American Literary Review* 22, no. 43 (1999): 19–30.

Valenzuela, Luisa. *Libro que no muerde.* Mexico: UNAM, 1980.

Van der Kolk, Bessel and Van der Hart, Onno. "The Intrusive Past: The Flexibility of Memory and the Engraving of Trauma." In *Trauma: Explorations in Memory.* Edited by Cathy Caruth, 158–82. Baltimore: Johns Hopkins University Press.

Verbitsky, Horacio. *El vuelo.* Buenos Aires: Planeta, 1995.

Walsh, María Elena. "En el país de Nomeacuerdo." In *Canciones para mirar.* Buenos Aires: Alfaguara, 2000.

Wannamaker, Annette. " 'Memory Also Makes a Chain': The Performance of Absence in Griselda Gambaro's *Antígona Furiosa.*" *The Journal of the Midwest Modern Language Association* 33, no. 3 (2000–1): 73–85.

Index

Page number in italics refers to illustration page

169

WITHDRAWN